IN PURSUIT OF BECOMING

one woman's journey to herself

SANDRA ASTACIO

In Pursuit of Becoming: One Woman's Journey to Herself
Copyright © 2018 by Sandra Astacio. All rights reserved.

No part of this publication may be reproduced, stored in a retrieval system or transmitted in any way by any means, electronic, mechanical, photocopy, recording or otherwise without the prior permission of the author except as provided by USA copyright law. Your support of the authors' rights is appreciated.

Unless otherwise noted, all Scripture quotations are taken from THE HOLY BIBLE, NEW INTERNATIONAL VERSION®, NIV® Copyright © 1973, 1978, 1984, 2011 by Biblica, Inc.® Used by permission. All rights reserved worldwide.

Interior Design | Cover Design
DHBonner Virtual Solutions LLC
www.dhbonner.net

ISBN: 978-0-578-46487-9

Published in the United States of America

IN PURSUIT OF BECOMING

one woman's
journey to
herself

To my blood of my blood, flesh of my flesh; my son, Brandon Aaron.

Your grace, love and understanding of who I was, who I am and who I was always meant to be has inspired me to keep pushing forward. May my love for God now inspire you to raise your children in His perfect way, knowing that His path for your life and theirs is paved with many blessings that He has set in place long ago! A strong, vigilant and faithful man of God you are; a prophet and soldier for Christ you are to become!

God bless you, son. I am so proud to be your Mother and the Grandmother to our baby Silas that you have made me to be!

~ Momma

CONTENTS

My Prayer for You, My Son 9
In Pursuit of Becoming...A Dialogue 13
Breathing Life 17
It's More than That... 19

IN PURSUIT OF BECOMING
a Proverbs 31 Woman

Introduction 25
Daughters In Christ 25
Proverbs 31:10 29
Proverbs 31:11-12 33
Proverbs 31:13-19 41
Proverbs 31:20-21 49
Proverbs 31:22-24 57
An Intermission: An Expression Of Joy! 65
Proverbs 31:25 71
Proverbs 31:26 77
Proverbs 31:27-31 85
Firsts 91

IN PURSUIT OF BECOMING
a Praying Woman

Introduction 97
Why Do I Pray? 97
Prayers Of Petition 105
The Prisoner 111

Prayers Of Deliverance..113
Prayers Of Intercession 119
Prayers Of Consecration And Purity: A Personal Testimony................129
Prayers Of Thanksgiving And Supplication 139

IN PURSUIT OF BECOMING
a Serving Woman

Introduction...151
Why Serve?..151
Her Son 153
Serving Him Through Our Family.. 157
Serving Him Through Our Church..167
Serving Him Through Our Work... 175
#FaithWalker...185
To Our Soldiers of War 191
Dear Daughter 195

Epilogue...197
About the Author...201

MY PRAYER FOR YOU, MY SON

I pray Love for you

Love will always be close in your heart, motivating you to always give more than you receive...

Love carries you through dark times, knowing that the kind of love that is given to you is unconditional, unyielding, and unending...

Love that fills every corner of your heart and makes you whole...

Love that leaves you open to more-allows you to be accepting to those that wish to give to you, share with you, and involve you in their world...

Love that is bold. It never shies from being seen, expressed or fought for. You wear this love as a badge on your sleeve for all to see, carrying it with pride...

I pray Acceptance for you...

Acceptance by all who are in your world to welcome you as you are, appreciating your gifts, your heart....

Acceptance of others on how they choose to love you, honor you, or hate you. If they choose to hate you, accept this truth and forgive them...

Acceptance of the things you cannot change. Understanding that we must live with things being just so, and we are powerless in changing it. Be ok with that...

Acceptance that there is a Greater Power than you. That it is open to you always. It loves you and accepts you as you are, no matter what you have done and how far you have gone...He will always be there....

I pray Peace for you...

Peace within you to stand for what you believe in...

Peace within you to know that not everyone has this within them... shine in their presence and you may cast that light that they need....

Peace that your soul is taken care of. It is full of love, acceptance, and honor and, as with peace, it is powerfully quiet...

That you bring peace to all disorder around you or have enough inside you to know when to walk away...

Peace within your mind to sit still and soak in what is surrounding you...

I pray Strength for you...

Strength that is not seen...but felt in all you do, heard in all you say...

Strength that allows you to be humble, to admit when you are wrong or when you are lost...

Strength to weather hard times, feel your way through it all- knowing that you must feel the pain to truly appreciate the good, the lesson...

Strength to hold the ones you love close when they need you...when they have fallen and cannot get up without your help...

Strength to say goodbye when you really don't want to but must.

Strength to stay...

I pray Wisdom for you...

Wisdom to know that there exists a difference over accepting what can't change and the strength to change it...

Wisdom to share your past with the right one...trusting your head and your heart at the right time...

Wisdom to stop making the same choices that hurt you, hurt others, or leads you to a place that would not make me proud...

Wisdom to walk away from the wrong thing at the right time...and not look back...

Wisdom to know that just because something is given to you, it can't be taken away....

IN PURSUIT OF BECOMING...
A Dialogue

"Odd title...seems like you are reaching for some pretty high goals there," I've heard them say. "Yes; yes, I am," I replied. Isn't that the God we serve? Pushing and pulling us to a higher realm that we can't even remotely imagine. A high goal that is only achieved when we are called Home, but while on Earth, motivates us to move strategically, cautiously, obliquely at times, but also with the blessed assurance that Abba Father has our hand. Wow! Just wow.

My Heavenly Father let me sink to the bottom of my own pit until I decided that living for Him was the only option for me. Living without Him was going to have me lying face in the dirt soon...very, very soon and that dead end was no place for a Daughter of the Most High to be.

Allow me to make this statement, "I follow Him only, not man, not a church, not an idea, not a group, not a fool, not a fancy, not a hot head, not a callous heart, not a broken pot, not a toiled hand that serves only itself, as most idled hands do." I have learned a great deal in these past ten years that I have since rededicated my life to Christ and the one thing that I will never make an apology for, is consistently beckoning His voice to move me out of the place I am! (Keep moving) I know that the God I serve will move me into my "next" where, and He will come alive to someone in my path. And that someone may even be me!

Hallelujah, praise God!

This journey to myself has shown me what God has grafted inside me. A hallowed ground of sorts that both confession and repentance lead to deliverance so profound that it has no choice but to be broken up into segments!

My deepest resolve of fear began early in life and to date, even as I type this very introduction, I am riddled with the notion that there will still be a session or two to come that even a deeper revelation will transpire. Over this keyboard, the very dreams that have come to lay dormant will begin to manifest. Over this keyboard will be a sanctified time of rebirth that only the one True God can ordain. Over this keyboard, this journey continues, and I am humbled that you have chosen to explore what He has revealed to me over time. Honored that out of all the things you could be dedicating time to, you have chosen to follow a prompting to read this compilation.

I am grateful and accept the blessing you have shown me. I also take on the responsibility of accurately reflecting the Father's heart and being biblically sound in any doctrine I share. **Luke 12:48** – "From everyone who has been given much, much will be demanded; and from the one who has been entrusted with much, much more will be asked."

Look, the journey has been painful and long. It has left scars that only my Heavenly Father can see, but it has also hewn hope, perseverance, enlightenment, and healing. All of which is far from over, but at least I'm at a point where I can share His glory in my life!

As you explore the pages to come you will find a mixture of biography, testimony, and impartation of the Spirit through writing series and much more. Sometimes a Father needs to impart words of wisdom, revelations of times gone by, lessons learned because of his own choices, advice on how to proceed on her own or other times, or just pour into her spirit a love and acceptance that only he can!

Often, a daughter needs her father to stand by her side when no one else is and help her remember how strong she really is. At times, he just shows her his heart and, silently, she observes. My Heavenly Father poured expressions of His heart into my Spirit and I now share them with you.

Step through the pages and witness the journey that I have taken to not only myself, but also a journey in a relentless pursuit of becoming all that He has created me to be!

May the Spirit of God move you and the hand of God richly bless your soul.

~ *Pastor Sandra*

BREATHING LIFE

Music was always playing in this quaint little wooded corner of this small town. A lonely street that many did not even know existed was home for a group of six families for generations to come! A neighborhood without fences, without walls and without locks on the doors all times of night. They spent holidays together, celebrated each other's birthdays, and held parties for no reason other than to celebrate life! The innocence, the unity, the family stories...multiple chapters and tragedies are embedded in those very woods even to this day.

Memories held onto by only a few of us now; but only one memory would set the tone for a life paced with heartbreak, abandonment, and emptiness.

A life where breathing has always been challenging.

The morning was still fresh as the breeze slowed through the back screened door, filling the little house with an aroma of honeysuckles, gardenias, and fresh cut grass. A pot of something delicious was boiling on the stove for later that day and the feeling of preparation was always in the air! Anticipation for the time, as a family, they can sit at the table and thank God for His blessings. The far-off sound of a car engine revving up can be heard and the very distinctive laughter of older men mixed with Spanish accents pepper the air.

Then, piercing the very same air were screams of terror! A screened door flew open, slamming onto the aluminum siding, shattering all stillness within an earshot. She emerged panic- stricken, fear meeting her tear-filled eyes as she held the lifeless infant in her hands! Soap bubbles up her elbow, her apron drenched with water and running down the front of her housedress, she held up the little girl, screaming, "Dios! Dios!"

Only two lawns away, the men could hear her screams above the engines and sprinted to her side. Without hesitation, one of the men started up the car and pulled into the yard, flinging open the passenger side door as he barely came to a stop. The women all gathered in that same instant to help her not to drop the soap- covered baby as she struggled to hold herself standing. As the man reached for the baby, she collapsed into the arms of her friends!

Then, one of the men pulled up the baby's little face to his and whispering something over her, cupped his mouth over hers, breathing LIFE back into her! Flipping her over, her mouth drained the water and then, she began to cry. Wrapped in a simple kitchen towel, he swaddled her close, hopped into the car, and rode away to the hospital on the other side of town.

My father breathed life into me then and continued to do so throughout my life until the very end of his own.

Therein lays a very dramatic beginning of a life filled with more moments of near drowning, breathlessness, and the resuscitative power of my Heavenly Father restoring the very air I need!

I'll never know what happened in that small kitchen that morning and how I came to be lifeless in the hands of my mother, but I do know that beginning with my earthly father, my dependency on a strength outside of myself, was imminent. Relying on my own wisdom was a recipe for disaster, but as God would ordain it, He allowed me to reach the end of myself before pulling me into the hope He had laid out for me.

IT'S MORE THAN THAT...

You heard all the things I said and saw the doubt in my heart.
You stood at the edge of the room and watched me in my darkest hours doubt, You.
You listened to my cries in the middle of the night as I summoned death to take me- make it all stop!

As I went from hand to hand...empty embrace to cold kiss, back into the unfamiliar arms of the next, You offered the comfort of Your wings...

Piercing holes burrow in my heart as I imagine the worst happening to my own flesh and blood... wondering how I arrived at this place of verdict with You.
Yet, I did not hear Your voice.

It came to me one day as I faced the carpet... what if? What if it is real? What if it is **not** a temporary fairy tale to hold onto for the short-sighted future?

Something to stop the pain...
For now.

What was there to lose that I had not already lost? My pride. My heart. My tears. My dignity. My own blood...

Lifting my eyes- my hands- my heart- my soul (whatever was left of it that I had not sold already), I cried out to You.
"Ok! Ok! - I give up!" The years of torment, guilt, shame, anger, bitterness...lost dreams.
Closeness, intimacy, love. What was that?! But, You offered it to me.
I opened the gift...

Then, layer by layer-the roots surfaced-but, not in the fire red color they once were. As they unearthed themselves from deep within my soul, You gently wiped away the dirt. My tears fell upon Your hand as You did this...but You didn't mind.
You revealed to me the reason.

"Now?" I asked. You said, "Yes, now."

Like watching it out of a rear-view mirror, the scenes became smaller and smaller...away. Looking forward, the path is narrower, but lit. A thousand lights! May I step forward?

It all looks different now. The dreams that I used to say would make me so happy...they are only wisps now. And maybe...they have come true. Maybe what You had planted deep in my heart that I used to laugh at because they were for someone else.
These are mine...a gift from You.

The promises that You made...the gifts You left for me at my heart's door. The gift of grace. The mercy! The mercy!
My covering now...it is the only thing that is red. The Holy Blood.

If any of them should ask me, "Is this new Love of yours all what we hear it is?", the response would be simple...

"It's more than that."
Hallelujah, it's more than that!

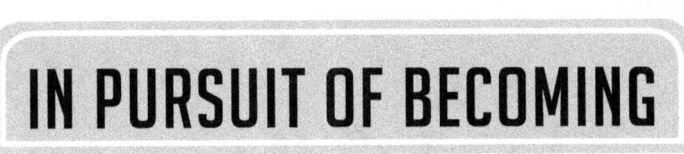

IN PURSUIT OF BECOMING

a Proverbs 31 Woman

INTRODUCTION
Daughters in Christ

$\mathcal{M}$Y REDEDICATION CAME AT a time of my life when rights of passages were met. My son was off to war, having joined the Army (much to my displeasure) and was serving a tour of duty in Iraq. My very identity was founded on being his mother – a messed up version of what I thought a mother should be – but, nonetheless, *his mother!* Divorced for the second time, living on my own in a town where there was not much to offer to the single woman other than nightclubs and over-the-top doses of 'culture' that left me even more confused over who I was. Confusion from sexual bondage, promiscuity, and addictions that robbed me of the very morality that I should have had raising my son. Although I functioned (holding jobs, paying my rent, establishing credit, etc.), there were periods of darkness that I faced demons head on, came face-to-face with certain death, and hitchhiked the highway to hell on weekends! The maddening circle of dysfunction was where I found myself and the pain of being empty was too much!

A friend of mine at the time took me to church. I went openly and eagerly. I listened. I prayed and felt something 'shift' for the first time in my direction that didn't resemble anything that I had seen before.

Salvation. True salvation.

I raised my hand and from there the journey to myself began. I joined the church, jumped into as many of the spiritual development classes as I could, and began reading God's Word. I was still living in the world and trying to find my way to negotiate this new beginning with my former self because making them mutually exclusive of one another didn't seem like an option at that time. Little did I know that they were, in fact, two radically different lives and the God which I had pledged my allegiance to understood me intimately. He knew me so well that He stood by patiently and waited for me to surrender wholly to Him and then He took care of all the purging from my life that I was too weak (and inexperienced) to complete myself.

The people, places, things, jobs, habits, speech, conversations, etc. ALL of it! He made it happen.

Soon I came to a place where I knew I would bloom! I would write a book! Not just any book, but a book of my story. My awful, prideful, angry, belligerent, adulterous, hedonistic, idol-worshiping, and self-serving story complete with recounts of debauchery, abuse at the hands of a family member, occult practices, rage-filled narratives of a woman scorned, and so much more! Here was my chance to heal my way through 30+ years of torment, dysfunction, and abandonment. If my family be named, then so what? If someone gets angry that I exposed them, then so what? I was in a decade-long fight with my Dad, and my Mother was so locked up in her own life that she wouldn't have noticed anyway, so why not?

So I fired up the laptop and began.

Until I heard, "Stop." I looked around and I was the only one in the room. I heard then, "You will not write unless it is for My Glory!"

I knew Who it was, and I knew why He said that; instead, I was asked to write an apology letter to my Dad, letting him know of my life change and let him know how much he was missed. Yes, deeply and honestly missed.

So I did just that. I wrote to my Dad. I sent a few pictures and I remember standing at the mailbox with tears flowing down my face, thinking to myself, "What if Dad doesn't care and doesn't write back?" All the emotion, tears, and crying out to God to help heal me in the past would be for nothing? Really?

But, just like that, I let the envelope go. I felt a sense of trust in God that I never experienced before, and I waited. Within a week, I got a letter back. I have it here in my home office and it is framed along with a picture of me kissing his sweet cheek. See, that one act of obedience began it all.

The pursuit of being healed from the past and entering the road of forgiveness forever changed the course of *both of our lives*! Soon after the exchange of letters, a couple of phone calls, I met my Dad after eleven years.

I didn't just see my Dad. I saw a redeemed, sanctified, Christ-loving man who changed his whole life years before to follow God. Wow!

My church at the time requested me to begin writing a single's blog for them but, within a year's time, disbanded the single ministry and I ventured out on my own. I named *Daughters In Christ* as a title to my blog and years later, made it into my own ministry.

The very first series of the blog is entitled "In Pursuit of Becoming a Proverbs 31 Woman." In the pages to follow, you will see how God leveraged my past as I explored what kind of woman I was grafted to be and how I redefined myself, despite the pressures of the world and what *they defined me as!*

In this first series, join me while we explore what becoming a Proverbs 31 Woman means. Let's look at how God ordains this definition as found in scripture and how we can begin to see ourselves, little by little, as noble, confident, strong, wise, and faithful Daughters in Christ!

> *"Charm is deceptive and beauty is fleeting, but a woman who fears the Lord is to be praised!"*
> **~ Proverbs 31:30**

PROVERBS 31:10

"A wife of noble character who can find?
She is worth far more than rubies."

Sometimes defining our own self-worth brings up the challenge of purposeful self-discovery. Some find this whole process or the very mention of it painful. It would mean uncovering layers of long-standing beliefs, deeply engrained in us from years of experience.

At times, these beliefs can be healthy, rooting confidence and self-esteem from an early age. Other times, it can be a series of lies that we were told from our youth that, frankly, we did not have enough energy or evidence to prove otherwise. As a young woman, I faced the pressure to be thin, dress right, have the in-style technology, and be an all-encompassed, powerful, self-reliant, SINGLE woman! After all, secular society glorifies the strong woman of today, making them icons in our businesses, icons in trend setting, and icons in entertainment!

How could I ever possibly add up to the world's definition of what my 'worth' should be? Lucky for me, God had an answer...

Did you know that rubies throughout centuries were often regarded as a symbol of freedom, unwavering dignity, and divine power? Interestingly enough, when we exam the definition of the word noble – "of exalted rank; of or pertaining to the nobility; distinguished from the masses by birth, station, or title" – we may be able to start seeing a connection. Does God really see us being distinguished and set apart? Yes, He does!

To help truly receive this from God, our internal standards for ourselves need to radically change. We can no longer hear the lies of the enemy or allow ourselves to be compared to one another. We must see ourselves in the mirror that God places before us! That mirror lies within the mind and our exalted rank begins with what we believe to be true in our own minds.

Scripture tells us that God made us in His image! In His image means our thoughts that later become our speech must be in line with giving Him glory!

Refrain from judgment, gossip, and lies. Realize that our beauty comes from our character, which is formed by our actions and beliefs. Our nobility rests within that same character that is formed!

We find in scripture how God's plan for us began before birth. As in **Psalm 139:13-16**, *"My frame was not hidden from you when I was made in the secret place. When I was woven together in the depths of the earth, your eyes saw my unformed body. All the days ordained for me were written in your book before one of them came to be."*

So careful to sculpt you in His own image, how could He not value you highest above all things He created? His love and your worth to Him are infinite! Is it no coincidence that the net values of rubies depend on both its color and weight, but more importantly, its place of origin?

God loves you. He values you, has plans for you, cherishes and delights in you. He desires for you to have a clear understanding of your worth, not by the world's deceptive definition, but by His truth! When you come to redefining your image in the mirror God has in front of you, a light will radiate from you that all others will see. The light of truth will illuminate in your words and in your actions.

A very distinct glow will happen in your soul that a virtuous woman carries into every room she walks in. Matter of fact, this might be a good time to tell you one last fact about a fine ruby.

In the right light, some rubies have intersecting needles within the stone allow it to cast a luminous shadow. This shadow is often in the shape of a star!

How awesome is our God to create two highly-valued, worthy, and stunning designs? A brilliant ruby and a noble woman!

Let's Pray

Dear Father, I pray that any woman reading this who struggles with her own self-esteem begins to seek out your truth about who she is in You. Your desire for us is to be righteous, virtuous, diligent, productive, and sanctified creations! We enter Your word to feel Your presence and hear from You. In doing this, we strengthen our minds to guard us against the things that are not of You! We are not to listen to the lies of the enemy, which can be in modern media, echoes of the past, or judgmental bias of what Christian women are to look like.

May Your merciful grace indwell us and fill our hearts with the hope to redefine ourselves by Your standards alone! Our worth to You is never changing and knows no end. Help us to remember that and regardless of Your sovereignty, You will draw near to us and change our hearts forever!

Thank you for loving us, your Daughters, and placing the highest value in us! As we strive to be of noble character, allow us to remain humble and pleasing to You.

Your certainty rises above all the chaos of our minds and we exalt You! In Jesus' Name...

Amen.

PROVERBS 31:11-12

"Her husband has full confidence in her and lacks nothing of value. She brings him good, not harm, all the days of her life."

*I*N CONTINUING WITH THIS series of examining The Proverbs 31 Woman, the next verses are **Proverbs 31:11-12.** In these verses, the first thing that came to my mind was, "Well, wait a minute—what if someone reading this isn't married, then what?"

Well, good question! The truth is, regardless of your marital status, God desires us to continue to be the strong, confident, and obedient woman who He designed us to be! When we seek His wisdom in this, we unleash the strength and dignity established in this description of a "noble woman." Whether we are single or married, the attributes of a "noble woman" are in direct significance to God!

Let's look at a definition of confidence, we may see it broken up in four parts: belief in one's own abilities, faith in someone to do right, (referred to) a secret, and a trusting relationship.

Now having said that, allow me to establish these points:

1. *Belief in one's own abilities:* Regardless if you happen to have a significant other in your life who would be able to proclaim his confidence in you, what can you honestly say about the confidence you have in yourself? Do you nurture and cherish what makes you uniquely different? Have you taken the opportunity to find out, on purpose, who you are and what your spiritual gifts are?

   If you haven't taken the time to complete this type of assessment, I would strongly encourage you to! I would recommend getting connected in your local church's spiritual development ministry and further explore your individual gifts. Learn how God has created you to use these same gifts to honor and serve Him.

   Developing this type of knowledge about who God created you to be will help install an added confidence in yourself as a valued member of His church! God has confidence in you. He has faith that you will also remain confident in Him; stepping outside of what things have molded you to this point and boldly transform your heart and mind as He desires! Firmly believing in your abilities and gifts from that point will help renew your faith in the plans He has just for you.

   > *"For I know the plans I have for you,"*
   > *declares the LORD, "plans to prosper you*

> *and not to harm you, plans to give you hope and a future."*
>
> ~ **Jeremiah 29:11**

2. *Faith in someone to do right*: We looked at first establishing the significance of self-confidence. Would this, then, be a critical step before we can expect any type of confidence from a partner?

    I understand not everyone is seeking a partner; however, for us to truly move into a place of understanding God's order and desire for us all, we must consider that being in a healthy, God-filled relationship is what has been spoken of since Genesis. (**Genesis 2:18**, *"The LORD God said, "It is not good for the man to be alone. I will make a helper suitable for him."*)
    But please also consider that if God's will for us is to not have a relationship, we must have the confidence in God that He is sufficient enough! God will always 'do right' for His children and remain sovereign in all areas of our lives, if we allow Him! We can have faith in Him to establish order from chaos, joy from pain, and strength from brokenness!

3. *(Referred to) A secret*: What is the secret that God whispers to you? Are you actively listening to Him override the lies of the enemy? He is speaking TRUTH into your life, Sister! He is entrusting you to be faithful in following Him, obeying Him, and living by His principles He has already established for your life. He has confidence in your ability to stand on the rock of His love, armored by the grace of His power!

This same power will be used to fulfill His will for your life! Knowing that He has this type of confidence in you to share such amazing truth should give you an unshakeable assurance in all you do!

4. *A trusting relationship*: This final part of the description is a result when you have confidence in yourself and in our Lord! It is also something that each one of us craves from all the relationships we have. Some of us have spent the better part of a lifetime attempting to have trust in anyone!

Taking much needed refuge in and leaning unto Him will help establish a relationship with God that He desires and help us in trusting others. With the strength of God's confidence in us, and our established relationship in Him, the fear that hold most of us back from trusting others is shattered!

Through seeing evidence of our trusting relationship with God, others will also see us as trustworthy. That's important, isn't it? After all, when others look at us, are they not to see Jesus in us?

Next, lacking "nothing of value" is a tall order as well, but when we realistically reset our priorities according to living a consecrated, sanctified, and purposeful Christian life, we intrinsically increase the value of our lives!

As I mentioned previously, we reinvent our surroundings and habits based on our beliefs. From these beliefs, we create our character! This noble character possesses the fruits of the Spirit and can be seen in our speech, our lives, and our efforts. These attributes, in of themselves, lack nothing of value!

> *"But the fruit of the Spirit is love, joy, peace, patience, kindness, goodness, faithfulness, gentleness and self-control.*
> *Against such things there is no law."*
>
> **~ Galatians 5:22-23**

Lastly, bringing someone "good" (and this includes yourself) may be thought of having a positive or desirable presence amid the pressures or demands of life. To bring a constant ray of light into someone's life would be a challenge at times, but with true restoration in Christ, strife, discord, and apathy become strangers to a changed heart.

Prioritizing to possess this type of respect for your own self-dignity and peace aligns you to attract the kind of partnership that God desires for you; one absent of harm and dysfunction. One that centers God in its definition, glorifying Him and empowering the finest attributes of a true Proverbs 31 woman!

Let's Pray

Dear Father, sometimes we get so consumed by what others see in us and their opinions that we forget that it is Your opinion of us that we must focus on. How we see ourselves in You helps us have a fuller and more satisfying confidence in our actions and beliefs. We must first be able to truly understand how You made us unique in ability and character and have that permeate every area of our lives. We can offer so much more to a life partner, a friend, a family member, ourselves, and more importantly, You!

We strive to become a woman of confidence and reverence in all we do! If we can be a woman that a man of Your choice would find worthy of depending on, having faith in, and actively support a trusting relationship, please favor us with such a relationship! If it is Your will for us, may we share a love with a man that centers You in all he does, but only In Your time, through Your will, and when You feel we are ready! Even if it not be in Your will, Lord, we proclaim right now that You are enough! You are sufficient in all we desire!

We request the Holy Spirit to reside within our very souls, bearing the fruits of His indwelling in all we do and say. We strive to lack nothing of value and allow our worth to be determined by only You. From all these things, we yearn to bring 'good' into the lives of people closest to us, into our own lives, and mostly to give You the glory. Mold us into the strong women You desire for us to be!

We thank You for continuing to guide us, Your faithful Daughters, and revealing Yourself to us more each time we call out Your name!

In Your Son's Holy name...

Amen.

A Glimpse...

The beginning of this series was over the span of many months. During the time of writing it, I went through a true hardship of heart! Not only was the time marked by sending my only son to war and realizing the magnitude of life, but it was also marked with a budding relationship that was burning with sin!

I had to take several steps back during this season to realign myself. I was lukewarm, still back sliding, and being a lover of self! I embarked on a very dangerous and heart-wrenching relationship with a man, who I fought for the hardest I have ever fought for anything in my life! Trouble was, he wasn't fighting for me!

The hard reality of addiction, sin, and blasphemous behavior took its final toll. I could not see overcoming these hurts on my own and cried out!

That is where He met me. In that moment of surrender! I looked up and asked why I was not fulfilled and tried to bargain my future with the Almighty God. I asked for Him to send me a man, like King David, that was after His very heart! In those still moments after launching such a tall order, I recall hearing in my spirit, "What if I don't? Am I enough for you?"

Stuttering and broken, I hesitated to answer Him clearly.

"Am I enough?" echoed in the air.

Finally, "Yes. Yes, Lord; You are."

PROVERBS 31:13-19

"She selects wool and flax and works with eager hands. She is like the merchant ships, bringing her food from afar. She gets up while it is still dark; she provides food for her family and portions for her servant girls. "She considers a field and buys it; out of her earnings she plants a vineyard. She sets about her work vigorously; her arms are strong for her tasks. "She sees that her trading is profitable, and her lamp does not go out at night. In her hand she holds the distaff and grasps the spindle with her fingers."

Over the past several months, I have observed many of my female friends' attitudes towards work, in general, and have found one common denominator – perseverance!

Regardless of their occupation, there stands this unyielding push to do the very best in all they do despite the circumstances. Whether it is in a customer service line of work where their environment is high-paced and demanding or it is more of an analytical position, calling for a steady focus measured by systems, the level of determination is the same. By examining the working woman within myself, I noticed that there is a sense of ownership about every facet of my job that I take very seriously. I wondered if I had taken some of these facets too seriously and if I would need a whole new perspective.

Researching scripture, I found:

> *"Whatever you do, work at it with all your heart, as working for the Lord, not for men, since you know that you will receive an inheritance from the Lord as a reward.*
> *It is the Lord Christ you are serving."*
>
> ~ **Colossians 3:23**

Wow! Knowing that my greatest audience is God Himself, certainly changed my perspective about my work! I believe that, as women, we are born with an innate sense of stewardship for the provisions that we are granted. As seen above in **Proverbs 31:13-19**, there are very definitive responsibilities listed for a woman from carefully selecting only the finest of things for herself and family to ensure that the resources are used wisely.

Verse 13 uses the word "eager" to describe her hands. When was the last time you were eager to work?

For me, anytime that I complete a task either at work or at home, the sense of accomplishment makes me feel great. But I had to ask myself if I stop to take notice of God *giving* me the strength to complete these tasks *every* time?

Well, honestly, no, not *every* time!

When reading back over this passage, I realized that God's desire is not just for me to be eager to complete the tasks at hand successfully, but to also be grateful for the strength that He manifested in me in the first place!

Being more conscience of this lately has given me even greater satisfaction in my work and, honestly, yielded even better results! I have noticed a pronounced focus and attention to detail that I did not have before.

Unfortunately, there is still some work-related stress, but in the perspective that God desires for me to have, I must instead focus on the end-goal and know that God will guide me. I am bound to have success with His direction!

Reading the remaining verses made me consider that maybe being diligent is still not enough. Perhaps I must be a bit more strategic in my work as well. Allowing this to really minister to my soul, I realized that although I am productive and will accomplish the more important things first, I will often lose sight of the smaller tasks. Basically, I don't always have a strategy!

In the book of **Proverbs 13:16**, it is written that *"A wise man thinks ahead."* Appreciating these words of wisdom, I have enacted a plan to ensure that *my* plans are aligned with *His* word and task by task, I will execute it!

Like the woman described in these passages, she works diligently and through wisdom makes sound decisions for her well-being and for the well-being of those entrusted to her care. She makes careful decisions that yield her profit and accomplishes what she sets out to do.

She is referred to as a 'merchant ship.' Merchant ships are extremely sturdy and are used to transport cargo and passengers during peace time. They are designed to withstand great weights, as well. As a woman, I know that my shoulders, too, withstand a great deal at times, but rejoice as I know that it is He who carries me and lightens my burden!

> *"Cast your cares on the LORD and he will sustain you; He will never let the righteous be shaken."*
>
> ~ **Psalm 55:22**

Now, with all this said, why is it still so easy for me to fall victim to whining about my long day or the added responsibilities I have?

I often wonder if I am in the wrong line of work, or if I am not being regarded/respected as I should, or if my boss has it out for me. Ugh! If I know that God has granted me the strength to rise each day with the provision of time and resources He has bestowed upon me, then I should not just be more grateful, I need to ACT IT!

It is not that I *have to* work; it is that I *get to* work! God has granted me the position that I hold with my company and the provisions I need to make ends meet! It is not that I *must* get up early to get ready for work and still manage a household; it is that I *get to* awaken early and set the tone for the day by being a caregiver and a reliable guide for my family.

Being more responsible with God's precious gift of labor is my main goal from now on. As stated in **James 4:15**, *"Instead, you ought to say, 'If it is the Lord's will, we will live and do this or that.'"* I will ensure my goals will always include a submission to God first!

Writing this has taken some time for me to complete as I was so convicted by His truth on this subject, that my own revelations led me to a radical change within my heart!

My attitude and focus are no longer about seeking the applause of man in my work but remembering that my truest audience is our Father!

As with anything else that we set out to do in His name (like serving or witnessing to people), *working* with a careful purpose is giving Him glory! Remaining noble, ethical, honest, forthright, compassionate, discerning, and concise in our efforts – no matter what line of work we refer to – continues to magnify Him in all we do!

> *"Give generously to him and do so without a grudging heart; then because of this the LORD your God will bless you in all your work and in everything you put your hand to."*
> ~ **Deuteronomy 15:10**

So, my Sisters, allow me to leave you with this challenge...the next time that you are at work, whether it is at home or surrounded by 200 people in a call center, will you remember Who it is that you are truly laboring for?

Stop and thank Him for *choosing you* for this job and ask Him to grant you the strength and grace you will need to complete the task He has before you. Rejoice in knowing that He stands beside you all day long and will guide you through your difficulties. He will anoint you with the tenacity and focus you will need to do, not just to show up to meet the challenge but it will be enough to conquer it!

Striving to become all that He has asked us to be, may we all be seen by others as a formidable force – majestic in our might, yet holding a delicate grace with others while we work for not just what others may benefit from, but more importantly what His Kingdom gains from it!

Let's Pray

Father, I come before You today humbled by this truth that You have laid before me. How much of an ungrateful heart that we can have at times! Please have mercy on us as we may say that we cherish our homes, our families, our work, our belongings, yet continue to complain amid such enormous blessings! It is Your desire for us to be fruitful in our efforts and serve others first before ourselves, yet how often do we all forget?

As a Proverbs 31 woman selects the finest of things for her family and takes care of these things, allow us to be reminded that it was You who selected us as Your finest creations and continue to take such good care of us!

Grant us strength to have strong arms to work diligently into the night, awaken early, and not sacrifice anything of worth for our families. Lord, enlighten our minds with noble thoughts and wise decisions.

As we faithfully tithe, bless our portion to give us what we need and allow us to in turn, to bless others. May our hands never tire, and may our feet always remain on the path that You select.

Teach us, Father, what our role is for Your Kingdom and reveal to us the greater good to be done in our everyday tasks. Forgive us, please, for our moaning and cries when we get a little inconvenienced, and gently correct our focus!

As single women reading this today, please grant them biblical truths about provision and empower them to live abundant lives that are a direct reflection of Your love and their ongoing obedience to Your will. They are not alone, but some of their resources may be limited. Abba, please pour favor into their lives and gird them protection from the snares of the enemy, his lies about temptation, and grant them strength to focus!

The women who are reading this who are not single, but have added responsibilities, assure them that they do not labor in vain! God, grant them a peace that comes from Your presence, Your guidance in their lives, and a quiet knowing that You are in control, watching and rejoicing in their steadfastness! Let them each know today that You are pleased with them for pressing on in a world that leaves many of us discouraged and weakened by our burdens.

I pray we all remember the greatest Servant of all, Your precious Son, our Christ Jesus! Help us strive to have that same servant heart in all we do! Thank you, Lord, for lightening our loads by allowing us to abide in You, fall safely in Your arms, and recharge our spirits to continue Your will! It is all these things, that I pray today in Your Son's matchless name...

Amen.

PROVERBS 31:20-21

"She opens her arms to the poor
and extends her hands to the needy.
When it snows, she has no fear for her household;
for all of them are clothed in scarlet."

*I*T HAS BEEN MY understanding for a long time that women are just natural nurturers. We, from a tender age, care for our dolls, our pets, our little brothers and sisters, or even sometimes our younger friends.

We learn that if you care for something deeply, that you *show it* in your actions and words. Whether or not that same type of care and attention was shown to us when we were just young girls does impact us as we grow older; however, as Daughters of a Most High God, we must work to heal and continue to foster this nurturing side of who we were designed to be!

You may be reading this thinking, "What does my upbringing or whether or not I have a nurturing side have to do with becoming a Proverbs 31 woman?"

Well, for starters, we must take into consideration God's two greatest commandments as shown in **Matthew 22:37-39**, *"Jesus replied: 'Love the Lord your God with all your heart and with all your soul and with all your mind. This is the first and greatest commandment. And the second is like it: 'Love your neighbor as yourself.'"*

What these verses say to me is that I am to love my God with ALL that I have and love others with the **same** passion!

After allowing this to really digest, I ask myself two questions: Am I really loving God with an infinite measure of adoration that He is so worthy of? and How do I focus my attention on loving others so that God would be honored in all I do?

First instinct is to say that ***I do*** love God with all my heart and all my soul and all my mind, but as I look deeper within myself, I feel a tugging at my heart; I can say that I love Him as I He has commanded, but I soon realize that my actions need to reflect the same.

Extending my hands to the needy has taken a few forms in my life. One, most obvious way, has been my involvement with homeless ministries in my local area. As I see the faces of these men and women who have been displaced due to a variety of issues, I quickly come to realize the depth of my heart. And even more intuitively, I realize the depth of <u>my gratitude</u>.

Examining my heart and gauging exactly how fortunate I am and how little I have shown gratitude makes me feel a bit ashamed. I go to the Lord and ask Him to forgive me immediately! I want to run home and throw my arms around my family and hold them tightly – praising God for their health and our abundance.

But, even the most repentant phase of my outpouring to Him, I can still see areas of opportunity in my own life that I must dedicate to fostering the care for the misfortunate.

> *"In Jesus, the service of God and the service of the least of the brethren were one."*
> **~ Dietrich Bonhoeffer**

The second form of extending my hands to the needy is how I serve my fellow man. Hard to imagine this, but are you aware of the alarming rate the working-class poor is growing in this country?

People just like us who are struggling to make ends meet, short-changing their health care or education just to put food on the table. I give abundantly to charity various clothing, household goods, shoes, etc. on a frequent basis. But still, in my heart, I know that is not enough.

I yearn to make a difference – not for my own satisfaction – but to give God the glory! For the one person out there, who may be giving up hope, may they see Jesus in action! A single mom praying for shoes for her kids, finds a pair at a local charity in great condition!

Our Lord knows every need and through me and you, He can have someone's prayer answered. I know this feeling as I raised my son alone; opting to give up much more than hope to survive at times. I remember the sting of tears on my cheek night after night... knowing that a faithful God will deliver... somehow... someway.

> *"Answer me when I call to you, O God of my righteousness. Give me relief from my distress; be merciful to me and hear my prayers."*
> **~ Psalm 4:1**

Serving either inside a church body or outside on the street needs to be met with the truest of heart. Too often I have seen women from all walks of life and ages serve in such a way that it clearly turns into an act of obligation or worse, legalism. I have seen bitter hearts feel that they were 'doing good works', so perhaps they will 'earn' the Lord's favor...missing out on the purest joy serving the Lord should lead to. Now, I know this same heart, because I have been guilty of it in the past. I thought in some way that the more I served, the more that my faith would be measured. Like somehow God has a measuring spoon dedicated to my works...winning me a seat in Heaven! How wrong I was!

> *What good is it, my brothers and sisters, if someone claims to have faith but has no deeds? Can such faith save them?* [15] *Suppose a brother or a sister is without clothes and daily food.* [16] *If one of you says to them, "Go in peace; keep warm and well fed," but does nothing about their physical needs, what good is it?* [17] *In the same way, faith by itself, if it is not accompanied by action, is dead.*
>
> ~ **James 2:14-17**

What the Lord has placed in my heart is this: Continue to place others before me, love them as I love myself, and walk knowing that I am worthy of such infinite love that needs to be given to others – <u>in its entirety</u>! Perhaps many of you may suffer with the same revelation at times but take heart that a most *definitive* God has an abundant amount of grace for us in times such as these! Amen!

The second part of this section of **Proverbs 31:21**, *"When it snows, she has no fear for her household; for all of them are clothed in scarlet"* also called to my heart in a mysterious way.

When I considered that scarlet was often been thought of as a fine cloth in Medieval Europe, I was intrigued to know more. I just knew this reference to scarlet in this verse held significance. I learned that scarlet was traditionally made by a unique weaving technique that made the cloth elastic by how the yarn (in most cases red in color) was twisted by hand. Because it was more durable in this form, it was often used for stockings and garments that fit tightly against the body.

By retaining heat and withstanding extreme cold, it was considered a luxury to have clothes made from it. Not only does the woman described in this passage have the desire to keep her family warm in the snow, she does so with the finest garment available! As God loved us enough to give us His Son as a sacrifice for our sins, this same passion of love is to be poured out to one another. After all, it is God Himself that we all yearn to please and, most importantly, continue to show Him how much we love Him!

From serving one another with the purest of hearts to nurturing other's needs by supplying them with the finest garments, a Proverbs 31 woman yields to a Godly order for her life – faithfully striving to adhere to His greatest commandments through all she not only believes in, but through all she does!

> *"The greatest among you will be your servant.*
> *Whoever exalts himself will be humbled,*
> *and whoever humbles himself will be exalted."*
> ***~ Matthew 23:11-12***

Let's Pray

Merciful Lord, I ask that You bestow upon us the humility that is required to truly receive this message contained in Your Word today. In our haste from day to day, we may be quick not to show our gratitude for what you have given us and, in that same haste, overlook those who have not been as fortunate.

You love us in such an infinite and immeasurable way and it is hard sometimes to be consistent in returning that same love to others. Soften our hearts to see through Your eyes and break those same hearts for what breaks Yours!

Extending our hands to the needy is what Your Son, Jesus, did. He never looked away when someone called out His name... Father, may we be that way!

With the guidance of the Holy Spirit, allow us to hear that still, small voice that whispers grace into our hearts when we are in the presence of the needy. We know that it is more than just saying that we wish them well, for it is Your will that we put forth the effort to help, to pray, to give hope and light to a people that may be lost in the darkness of their circumstance. May we speak truth over their lives and allow them to hear You through our voice!

Lord, may our hearts be pure to receive the uncontainable joy that comes from serving our fellow man. It is not by deeds, Father, that we earn a place beside You, but by our faith. Thank you for revealing to me where my faults are and giving me the heart to continue to serve You!

I pray for every beautiful woman who reads this have a stirring of her soul that will reap a Spirit-led effort to further extend her hands. I pray that the same peace, comfort, and shelter that comes from Your warm embrace be extended to their families and loved ones with a desire to please You, Lord! To give You the glory, honor, and praise that You are so deserving of...we love

You, our mighty and gracious Host. Please allow every Daughter, who is reading this right now, feel Your amazing presence.

Give her the strength and bravery to step forward in serving You with all she has, confidently carrying out Your will for all of us. Hear the deepest whispers within our hearts, Father, as we yearn to hear You say, "Well done, my Daughter." All these things I pray in Your Son's most exalted name...

Amen.

May He be seen through you.

A Glimpse...

During this next hiatus from writing, God granted me an amazing experience; I became engaged and married a man who I did not ask for, nor deserve! Do you remember earlier when God asked me if He would be enough and I said Yes?

Well, He sent this man to me to show me the amazing love of Christ that I had (unknowingly) been longing for my whole life. Our story is unique and one day, I am sure, the Lord will allow us to share it in detail, but what I can reveal to you is that it was certainly all God!

As our lives began to unfold into something that neither of us would ever dream of it being, we witnessed repeatedly the hand of God in the areas of our lives we surrendered to Him. The season represented next was marked with learning to identify His fingerprint in our lives and celebrating His faithfulness through unbridled joy and the deepest sorrow we would ever have to face!

PROVERBS 31:22-24

"She makes coverings for her bed; she is clothed in fine linen and purple. Her husband is respected at the city gate, where he takes his seat among the elders of the land. She makes linen garments and sells them, and supplies the merchants with sashes."

*W*HEN ASKING GOD TO reveal to me what He wishes for me to share, He never ceases to amaze me! He leads me to all sorts of supporting stories within the Bible that further deepen my understanding of selected Scripture.

When asking Him to help me relate the mentioning of 'fine linen and purple' to an applicable message, here is where He led me:

One of those listening was a woman from the city of Thyatira named Lydia, a dealer in purple

> *cloth. She was a worshiper of God. The Lord opened her heart to respond to Paul's message.*
> ~ **Acts 16:14**

In the book of Acts, a woman by the name of Lydia is referenced. She may have been a prosperous businesswoman herself as she dealt in purple cloth which was known to be worn by royalty. She was from an area that was noted for its production of purple dye, Thyatira, and was a woman who believed in God (Yahweh).

When she heard Paul's message about Jesus Christ, she not only chose to believe in Him, but also Scripture points us to the word "respond" to describe <u>her reaction</u> to the gospel! She reacted by immediate obedience to Him in baptizing and fostering Christian beliefs/actions in her home. She became someone who was charitable and a willing servant of God's church directly.

Resting on the color purple itself for just another moment, allow me to give you some words associated with it: *royalty, nobility, ambition, wisdom, dignity, independence, and creativity.* (Sound like attributes of a Proverbs 31 woman yet?)

Picturing the distinction of Lydia's business, the aura of prestige assumed by the purple cloth itself and the immediate response to what Paul was teaching, are you starting to get a feel for a momentum here?

> "Her husband is respected at the city gate, where he takes his seat among the elders of the land."
> ~ **Proverbs 31:23**

Now some of you may not be married, so I ask that you pay special attention to the word 'husband' as used in verse 23. When I mentioned before that God simply amazes me on specific revelations, He was exceptionally surprising here. As I was watching a very popular sitcom, the husband on the show was telling his wife that he is known by others through her actions. That in so many ways, he further explained, reflects <u>how</u> he is regarded to his community and this has a great deal to do with how **she** conducts herself.

Well, I can make the argument that this concept runs hand in hand with marriage itself, noting **Mark 10:8**, *"and the two will become one flesh. So they are no longer two, but one flesh,"* but what correlation can we make for the single women among our readers? Well, the answer was magnified all at once in my spirit: **Jesus!**

> *"The bride belongs to the bridegroom.*
> *The friend who attends the bridegroom waits*
> *and listens for him, and is full of joy when he*
> *hears the bridegroom's voice. That joy is mine,*
> *and it is now complete."*
> **~ John 3:29**

How we refer to Christ as our **bridegroom** is how we are to also regard Him in all we do! We regard Him as our significant other, offer Him esteem by exalting Him above all others and recognizing His place as royalty in our lives, our King of all Kings!

We listen for Him and are often filled with joy when we feel His touch! When I think of how I regard my husband and family (loving them unconditionally), I immediately relate it to the love I have for Christ! And more importantly, the love He has for me!

So how we regard God is seen through our actions! We know, as Christians, that not everyone feels the same way about God, so would it not be up to us to ensure that we are the correct image of His truest nature? Recently, a very wise woman of God told me that sometimes, we are the only Christ that some people see.

Maybe this is something to think about.

But, just as I mentioned how Lydia reacted to the gospel by her obedience in action, I am led to the last verse of our selected Scripture:

> *"She makes linen garments and sells them, and supplies the merchants with sashes."*
>
> **~ Proverbs 31:24**

There is ACTION in this verse! It contains three <u>separate</u> actions! I envision diligent detail in hand-stitching sashes for the merchants. This must have taken hours!

Placing action behind our devotion to God speaks volumes of who we are in Christ. It is one thing to be close to God and have a relationship with Him, but we must challenge ourselves by stretching beyond this. Personally, I had to look at my level of service. I had to look deeply at my actions and ask myself if they were truly honorable to God, do they align with what He desires for me, and most importantly, does it reflect His command in the Great Commission.

> *"He said to them, '**Go** into all the world and **preach** the gospel to all creation. Whoever **believes** and is **baptized** will be saved, but whoever does not believe will be condemned. And these signs will accompany those who believe: In my name they will **drive** out demons; they will **speak** in new tongues; they will **pick** up snakes with their hands; and when they drink deadly poison, it will not hurt them at all; they will **place** their hands on sick people, and they will get well.'"*
>
> **~ Mark 16:15-18**

I purposely bolded the verbs as they resonated in my spirit. I know that I must begin by applying ACTION to my faith! I am beginning this by making a list of all the things I should be doing to regard, esteem, and honor God in all I do. Below is a small portion of a very long list that I composed for myself:

- Pray to Him – always
- Trust in Him – always
- Believe Him – always
- Worship Him in all I do! (Singing isn't the only way to worship, by the way.)
- Represent Him to the lost (Be brave and bold like the Apostle Paul.)
- Reflect His love in my words and my deeds
- Seek Him for protection (Stop relying on my own strength!)
- Serve others
- Love others – always

So does it stop at your family and God? No! I encourage you, Sisters, to spend some time with the Lord today and recognize how you are thought of as royalty to our King! Commit to display regard and honor for your Bridegroom, Christ Jesus, through your love of others.

And lastly, ask Him to place the will within you to have ACTION behind your faith, obediently carrying out His Great Commission. I am confident that He will not only strengthen you as He quickens your spirit, but a reflection of His grace and beauty will certainly shine through you to others!

Let's Pray

Lord, it is with the humblest of hearts that I ask You to hear the silent whispers of the women reading this right now and comfort them. As women who eagerly search for the desires of Your heart, Lord, we sometimes miss the fact that we are Your Daughters and co-heirs with Your Son, Christ Jesus. We mistakenly speak ill of ourselves or allow the impact of our busy lives stop us from taking the best care of ourselves.

We are regarded as royalty to You, Father, and we must remain in that same nobility as we regard ourselves and others, loving them as You first have loved us. Lord, help us remind each other gently when we are not carrying out Your Great Commission and not honoring what it is You have commanded. You are our King, our Bridegroom, our subsistence and source!

May everything we say and do be a gentle reflection of Your love and grace. When we fall short, as we all do, we thank You for Your infinite forgiveness. We cherish You. We exalt You. We honor You. You love us with an agape love that defies our understanding. But, as we dedicate our time and hearts to You, we ask that You show us how to love this way, how to minister to others and how to be bold like Paul as we preach the good news across Your land.

Abba, it is within Your Spirit that these things can take place – as we are so limited within ourselves. However, through You, we are mighty and able. We are wise and careful. We are loving and gentle. May we find strength through You to put more ACTION into our faith! We know that faith without deeds is useless and we yearn to hear Your voice giving us praise as we make You proud!

Most Holy God, Your servants reading this now want to feel the burning inside their souls to move when You say move; stay when You say stay, and become known to You as a faithful Daughter. We do not wish for the praise of man, just the blessings and

> *favor that can only come from the One Whom created us in His likeness... You, our most righteous and holy God! I ask that You speak to those who seek to hear You today and enable them to live as a royalty among Your Kingdom here on Earth until the day You call us Home.*
>
> *Through the Holy Spirit, in the name of Your Beautiful Son, Jesus Christ, these things I pray on behalf of my Sisters in You...*
>
> *Amen.*

May our Heavenly Father join you as you continue this journey towards becoming more of a Proverbs 31 woman!

AN INTERMISSION:
An Expression of Joy!

"Be still and know that I am God…"
                              ~ **Psalm 46:10**

My BEAUTIFUL SISTERS,

I wanted to take this opportunity to share with you an experience that I had with God where I learned a benefit about 'being still.'

I have had the blessing of time to reflect lately and reconcile my hurts and disappointments to the Cross, and God has placed upon my very soul a stirring…a peaceful, yet, profound stirring. I have navigated both in and (unfortunately) out of His will for my life too many times! Like the faithful, loving God He is, He has welcomed me back each time with open arms! I am so grateful for the love that He shows me, for how He shows me and also even for WHEN He shows me…

I had the honor to attend a spiritual retreat and heard a message from God <u>directly</u> that split through the very marrow of my bones. As I was experiencing one of many unique displays of His agape love, I found myself on my knees, outstretched arms and a joyous (but quiet) laughter within my soul that literally shook my whole body! To feel His love in this way was simply...well, indescribable!

I was shown throughout this retreat the servant love of Christ through others. I was shown how deeply my closest friends and family felt about me – truly – what they SAW in me that God has accomplished. I was quietly and humbly brought to the reality that God's grace was alive in me and how He has used this willing vessel to touch others came full circle back to me. But it was when the hours of devotion, fellowship, prayer, Holy communion, and stillness accumulated that changed something within me forever...

As I bowed my head and sat in a beautiful, dimly lit chapel, I came face to face with the living Spirit of God Himself! I was thanking Him for each and everything in my life. I was petitioning Him to show me His will for not just my life, but His will for all things. I was asking Him for salvation for those closest to me. I was requesting of His continued mercy and grace for those lost...a lifting of the darkness for His land.

As I listened to His voice minister to my spirit and instruct me to MOVE in a specific area of my life, He gave me a glimpse of what was to come and beckoned me to follow... I felt a warm and calming peace resonate within my body and a joy overcome me! I wanted to stay in this feeling forever! I remember thinking, "Can I just stay right here, Lord?" and no sooner did I think that, I was quickened with an answer from Him, "You will."

Whoa! Goosebumps ran up and down my body and I began to laugh with a bliss that I STILL cannot equate to anything that I have ever experienced.

Having my son decades ago, falling in love with the man that God sent to me, being delivered from bad experiences, witnessing His movement in someone's life and in my own...although abundant joy poured (and continues to pour) out of those moments, nothing has compared, Sisters, to this amazing feeling!

I was experiencing His love; simple, unobstructed, uninterrupted, pure, breath-taking love. As I surrendered my body to feel and move as it wanted, I felt His overwhelming presence. Warmth. Glory. Truth and confirmation of my right-standing with Him. I remember exhaling.

It was when I said, "I will, Lord," that I began to open my eyes to see the ceiling of the chapel and feel the weight of my outstretched arms. I realized I had slipped from the pew to my knees! Laughing to myself, I just shook my head and whispered to myself, "So THAT is what I am supposed to feel! Hallelujah!"

Within moments, my retreat leader was by my side, embracing me and smiling. There, another beautiful vessel of His love sat right next to me! What an angel this woman is!

Sisters, know that I pray for the Spirit of God to speak to my soul in a way that will decrease my opinion and <u>increase His truth</u> before I write anything! I asked Him to give me the strength, the wisdom, the ability, and the time to finish this book and move to what He has in store for all of us.

My prayer is that you experience an unbridled and unedited moment of glorious JOY with your Creator today!

Let's Pray

Holy and most High God, I ask that Your presence and sovereign Spirit fall upon those who are taking the time to read about our time together. I ask that You manifest a moment of clarity and stillness among the beautiful women reading this now that profoundly changes them forever! Your agape love is so incredible and infinite, that only a moment of our time dwelling in It feels like eternity.

The Author of all time, please give each of these women an instance that magnifies Your Spirit. Thank You for all Your times of deliverance, joy, peace, provision, grace, favor, clarity, knowledge, truth, quickening and movement in our lives. Your abundant care for us humbles us...it leaves us speechless... it leaves us in awe of You time and time again. Thank You for this testimony and for the glimpse of Your most glorious face. How can I ever compare a moment in Your glory to any word within our finite understanding? Seek within us any self-gain and pull it from our spirits...may only all that we say and do bring You glory, God. When we fall short, as we often do, thank You for Your forgiveness!

A deserving and gracious Father You are... we humbly, yet joyously, surrender to Your will! Protect and gird us with Your strength to move forward, preparing the Way for Your Son, Christ Jesus, to bring Your People Home, one willing and yielded heart at a time! Hallelujah! Hallelujah!

In Your Son's Holy Name, above all names, we pray these things.

Amen.

A Glimpse

This spiritual retreat was a landmark event in my life; not only did I experience firsthand the agape love of Christ, but I also had the experience to hear God command me to pour into the life of my Dad! My Dad was a Christian, a faithful servant, missionary, and devoted husband.

When God gave me instructions, He was specific. He gave me a charge and I fulfilled it. As a result, my Dad relinquished his greatest apprehensions towards his faith, disbanded myths, and came to a place of wholeness with Christ only weeks before his passing.

It was through God's grace and unyielding favor in that season that I made it through the death of the first man who I ever loved – my sweet Dad. From that place of humble, new beginnings to forgiveness and realignment to His Word, both my Dad and I experienced an abundant joy so few experiences with family.

I miss my Dad more than words can say, but not a day goes by that I don't recognize God's imprint on my life in the shape of my inherited behaviors, humor, and love for Jesus.

Just like my Dad!

PROVERBS 31:25

*"She is clothed with strength and dignity;
she can laugh at the days to come."*

I HAVE MET MANY WOMEN who I would describe as strong Daughters of God.

I marvel at their way of dealing with unexpected adversities, devastating illnesses, sudden joblessness, and life-changing trials. I watch how they navigate through the deep seas of the unknown with an equally profound grace. I ask about the human side of their feelings: "How does it feel in the darkest of hours, the loneliness of moments when no words can describe your pain?"

Without blinking an eye, I get the answer, *"That is when I am the least alone – God is with me. I lean into Him. I cry out to Him and He hears me!"*

Although that truth I know now, I can admit to you that it was never that easy to shed my fleshly emotion and view my life through the eyes of Christ.

> *"Don't you know that you yourselves are God's temple and that God's Spirit dwells in your midst?"*
>
> **~ 1 Corinthians 3:16**

I recall a time earlier in my Christianity when I experienced a life change so profound that I was <u>convinced</u> that no one would ever be able to really empathize with me.

No one!

As I listened to the enemy tell me lies, I secluded myself physically away from other believers and before too long, found myself heading head-first into a depression. I remember hearing in a song, "Be strong in the Lord," and thinking to myself, "Ok, but *HOW*?!" (This is the same kind of faithfulness that these strong women of God have experienced time and time again.) Naturally, as women, we cannot help but feel secure in anyone or anything that shows that kind of consistency.

I began to pray; however, not as I usually did. This time, I prayed with a heavy petition for God to guide me. I wanted to know how to find strength in Him. I asked Him to show me a practical way to lean in and capture that same hope and peace which others felt. God spoke to me in my spirit and reminded me to be in His Word every day.

As I turned page after page, He began to reveal to me more of Him... His faithfulness and the unchanging love He has shown throughout generations. I read how He disciplined the ones He loved. I saw how He led His people away from certain death and delivered them from captivity. I read of His mercy extended to those who repented of their ways and dedicated their lives to following Him. I read how King David cried out to Him and yearned for forgiveness, consecration, and pureness of heart.

As he asked of God His favor, he also requested a spirit of strength.

The same strength that these women of God have indwelling in them; the kind that allows them to lean in during times of turmoil and uphold their grace to speak peace over unexpected situations!

> *"Create in me a pure heart, O God, and renew a steadfast spirit within me. Do not cast me from your presence or take your Holy Spirit from me. Restore to me the joy of your salvation and grant me a willing spirit, to sustain me."*
> **~ Psalm 51:10-12**

I concluded that the strength that comes from the Lord – *the indwelling power that resonates within the sinews of our souls* – gives us refreshing hope and the kind of steadfastness that David yearned for. Sustainable power that gives me the footing I need in times when the winds of change try to blow me over and shake me off my foundation!

> *"See, I lay a stone in Zion, a tested stone, a precious cornerstone for a sure foundation; the one who relies on it will never be stricken with panic."*
> **~ Isaiah 28:16**

As it relates to upholding my dignity in those times, I reflected upon the infinite grace that God bestows upon me. It is under my choosing to display this same grace during my times of challenge.

I examine the definition of dignity and see that it speaks of worthiness, honor, esteem, and reservation of speech, action, or appearance. I remember who I am in Christ – a noble woman who even during times of strife, does not forget that I represent Him! My dignity reflects my acknowledgment of what honor He has given me, and He deserves to be given glory for my strength at all times; especially, the hard ones.

I also believe what the Bible tells me about being joyous! Although we are human, we are to strive to find joy in our hearts when facing trials.

We must join in the laughter within our souls that stems from knowing of His promises of an eternal life. When we rest on His promises of hope and align our hearts to His, we can laugh at the days to come.

I know that His work within me prepares me for ministering to others during their times of need. I can have a deep assurance that the Holy Spirit intercedes my heartfelt prayers like David's and delivers me from a hopeless fear of the unknown.

> *"Therefore, since we have been justified through faith, we have peace with God through our Lord Jesus Christ through whom we have gained access by faith into this grace in which we now stand. And we rejoice in the hope of the glory of God. Not only so, but we also rejoice in our sufferings, because we know that suffering produces perseverance; perseverance, character; and character, hope. And hope does not disappoint us, because God has poured out his love into our hearts by the Holy Spirit, whom he has given us."*
>
> **~ Romans 5:1-5**

Let's Pray

My most faithful God, I ask of You to accompany the women reading this and minister to the deepest places within their hearts that may harbor fear of the unknown. These places have been occupied by the lies of the evil one and I request a complete indwelling of Your grace, mercy, and truth to reside there instead! As we find strength in You, trust in You, and surrender our lives to You, help us remain steadfast in our trials. Help us with our momentary unbelief that anything can overcome our issues and have mercy upon us when we fail to lean into You as we should.

We can be frail and scared of life's changes and become shortsighted of Your sovereign plan for our lives. We try to jump in and save ourselves, which only leads us to failure! Lord, Your heart is so pure, and we yearn to have one just like it. We wish to hear Your voice remind us of Your will for our lives lies within Your hands! Abba, give us a clear path and mold us to become the strong, dignified and joyous Daughters You have created us to be.

We stand on the foundation of Truth that You, alone, have created. We gain our footing on peace and the assurance of Your promises. Nothing can come against us, Father, as You are the Almighty force and power within us; girding us with the same power that rose Your Son from the grave.

Place a hedging of protection around my Sisters as they step forward with the hope and joy that comes from trusting in You, God. We love You, magnify Your glory in all things we do and say! Abiding in You, surrendering ourselves, and resting in Your promises, we pray.

In the name of Your Glorious Son, Christ Jesus, we beckon You.

Amen.

PROVERBS 31:26

"She speaks with wisdom,
  and faithful instruction is on her tongue."

Wisdom... we hear so much about it from society and typically it relates to subject matter gurus, Tibetan monks, or isolated historians of our times past. Frankly, I immediately get the image in my head of a hermit on a mountain-top and being one of those poor souls who trudge up a steep hillside to hear a profound word or two.

"Please, wise one, give me the answer to life!" I hear myself say to only turn back down the mountainside with a perplexed look on my face, trying to make some applicable sense of his ramblings.

Blessed are we who have a faith and trust in a High God who doesn't leave us to fend for ourselves over His mysteries. We relish the moments of whispered words from His Majesty's lips, as we know that He has spoken directly <u>to</u> us, <u>for</u> us, and in anticipation <u>of</u> us following His wisdom above our own (or anyone else's, for that matter).

We fall prone at His still voice, feeling overwhelmed by His interest in our hearts, our souls, our minds, our situations! And what's more, that He then fills us with the Holy Spirit to <u>apply</u> His words to our lives at that very second!

Hallelujah!

Sisters, I do not claim to know much of anything enough to be called an expert, but the one thing that I do *know* is what I have experienced at the hands of God Himself, I can be considered an authority of. His wisdom yields from my eventual obedience to His calling and forgoing my own stubborn viewpoint.

No matter how close I would get to living a life of piety for Him, I would stumble, get mad, try it my way and, well, lose horribly. Only to return to Him in repentance and with a gentle and gracious Hand, He would forgive me.

NOT repeating those lonely and misguided steps is where I birth wisdom!

> *"He who leans on, trusts in, and is confident of his own mind and heart is a [self-confident] fool, but he who walks in skillful and godly Wisdom shall be delivered."*
>
> **~ Proverbs 28:26**

He has furnished us with His Word; His living, breathing, inerrant, and complete Word! All the textbooks, self-help books, and motivational training in the world combined cannot even *come close* to the consistency and time-transcending Truth of the Bible.

Please don't get me wrong, I think that the age of motivational, self-help venues may still continue to exist in some cultures and even prove to be beneficial – at least on the surface, but the sustainability of God's Word far exceeds get-better-fast schemes or make-me-likable workshops that our society thrives on.

It is through grace, mercy, compassion, patience, kindness, self-control, joy, and most of all, love that builds the solid transformation of hearts and minds that is permanent. I have heard some claim that these attributes are somehow the cause of distress among people or that they somehow make man weaker and less able to defend themselves.

Quite the contrary to any true Christian! We know the Power that is within us is greater than any power that is against us. We walk in the confidence of our Lord and stand as more than conquerors! It is *without* Him or His word that we are weakened.

> *"He is wise in heart, and mighty in strength: who hath hardened himself against him, and hath prospered?"*
>
> ~ **Job 9:4**

There is no wrong answer to the life-giving truth of the Gospel. The wisdom we possess is pulled from the recesses of Scripture that we actively apply to our everyday life and model in our actions towards others. To me, it sounds simple, but rarely is it. We are constantly being formed, molded, and forged as images of Christ. Our greatest battle is with our own flesh and it can stunt that growing process!

When there are times of greatest war within my own mind, fighting the lies of Satan within my surroundings, I can only choose to lean in harder towards Christ. When these instances happen, there are pearls of wisdom available to me, if I would only choose to store them up. I must make a conscious and volitional decision to follow the Holy Spirit's prodding and however fearful, take a leap in faith. From these moments of victory, true wisdom is born!

> *"For the Lord gives skillful and godly Wisdom;*
> *from His mouth come knowledge and understanding."*
>
> ~ **Proverbs 2:6**

Leading others even during these times can be a bigger challenge than any of Webster's words could ever describe.

Amidst unfounded conjecture, hostile criticism, and shameless mockery at times, my actions are to display the humbleness of Christ. The wisdom of what He has shown me must dictate the faithful instruction that is to fall from my tongue. It is hard; I will be honest. The human flesh wants to take over those times and satisfy the inner pain that I am experiencing.

Instead, I must remember that when others see or hear me, that they are to see or hear *God*. I am far from mastering this one, but He knows my heart and my deep desire to please Him.

> *"Behold, You desire truth in the inner being;*
> *make me therefore to know wisdom in my inmost heart."*
>
> ~ **Psalm 51:6**

So, Sisters, allow me to end this piece by reminding you that we all have sinned and fallen short of the glory of God (Romans 3:23), but by humble repentance and consistent prayer, we can work towards becoming the Godly women that Jesus is depending on to be His hands and feet in this world!

Against the wiles of the enemy and the destructive trend our society is quickly spiraling towards, we must match these same forces with a wisdom that has stood the test of time. From the Author of all time, we must endure the final days of His prophecy with a steadfast unyielding to the influences of our inner worlds.

There is only one solution. There is only one defense. There is only one victory...**His wisdom.**

Seek it with all your heart.

> *"If any of you is deficient in wisdom, let him ask of the giving God [Who gives] to everyone liberally and ungrudgingly, without reproaching or faultfinding, and it will be given him."*
>
> ~ **James 1:5**

Let's Pray

Holy God...as Your humble servant, I come to You today to ask You to hear my prayer. To help forge me into the woman You have designed me to be. To walk with humility, but power. To speak with gentleness, yet with conviction. To teach with wise instruction yet warn sternly. To help me to pray for the things that You desire for me, giving me insight to Your will for my life.

Impart the Holy Spirit to guide me through times of turmoil and strife. To reveal to me pearls of wisdom in my circumstances. These same Truths to be later spoken over those whom You bring into my life. Instruct me, Lord! Be among Your chosen people that have read these words that You have placed in my heart today and guide them.

They yearn to be searched, O' my Heavenly Father, and purged of the desires of the flesh. The same flesh that we have fought against since that time in the Garden...forgive us when we do not yield to the wisdom that You have so graciously bestowed within us...Thank You, Abba.

Hallelujah, My Lord, for Your grace...Your mercy so true... mold us to walk in Your Light and share with others the wisdom that comes from the only true Source of all knowledge. It is in the Name of Christ Jesus I pray these things with the love and promise of eternal Life with You.

Amen.

A Glimpse...

As I mentioned before, there was a time that I was separated from my Earthly Dad and in my own stubbornness, created a chasm of unknowing about my Dad, his life, and what God had called him to do during those years. I have coined that block of time as 'the lost years.' I sought out multiple avenues to fill the large gap in my heart that I believed was caused by unforgiveness, apathy, feelings of abandonment, rejection, disappointment, just to name a few!

What God ordered me to do, reaching out to my Dad, began a healing journey within me! I was a willing participant in this process and worked hard to boldly face the reality of my memories, discerning the facts from the fiction within my own mind.

This last segment of In Pursuit of Becoming a Proverbs 31 Woman is a dedication to the woman that, at this time, had been married to my Dad and the person she showed herself as being during that time. Unfortunately, soon after my Dad's passing, our relationship ended abruptly.

See, among the times that God was at work and showing me His glory during this most challenging time, Satan was on post, as well. He used her then and sadly, even to this day, to veil my Dad's wishes and isolate his surviving family forever. Betrayal, rejection, abandonment, and hateful intention surfaced; however, unlike before, Jesus is Lord of my life and the afflictions are only temporary.

On behalf of my Dad's beloved family, we are standing on His promises and know that He has the final say. We worry and fret not. We forgive and move forward; harvesting the fondest memories of our Dad and rest in the assurance that we WILL see him again!

PROVERBS 31:27-31

"She watches over the affairs of her household and does not eat the bread of idleness. Her children arise and call her blessed; her husband also, and he praises her:

Many women do noble things, but you surpass them all. Charm is deceptive, and beauty is fleeting; but a woman who fears the LORD is to be praised.

Honor her for all that her hands have done, and let her works bring her praise at the city gate."

As I draw a close to this series of Becoming a Proverbs 31 Woman, I would like to share a very personal story about how God's inspiration for this season of my life began. Little did I know at the time of our reuniting, that God was already at work in the lives of both of my Dad and his bride and that their obedient love for the Lord would guide me through one of the most traumatic times of my life.

For about eleven years, I was estranged from my father. It was mostly due to pride on both of our parts, but primarily because God was not in the *center* of our lives. During those years, God worked on both of us independently, showing each of us the lives that He truly designed for us to have.

He delivered both of us from sinful and worldly ways, addictions, negative thought patterns, etc. He gave to us another chance – *a last chance* – of restoration and healing.

Also during this time, He brought my Dad a beautiful woman. To my Dad's blessing, God grafted into her heart, as well, a newness of spirit and a rededication to a Godly life.

At the prompting of the Lord, I reached out to Daddy about two years before he passed away. To my delight, he reached back. From that time, God gave us the restoration and healing that both of our hearts and souls so desperately needed. The Lord continued to work in both of our lives and over the final year of his life as my father suffered a great deal of physical pain and suffering from his back, in addition to many other ailments.

My sweet father was weakening right before my eyes. But no matter how much he suffered, he would always give praise to God as he knew of God's promises and that someday soon the Lord he worshipped would fulfill those same promises!

And there she was...his bride. Noble, honest, loving, gentle, kind, patient, merciful, and diligent. Streams of tears fell from her face when she would speak of how much her faithful and loving husband was suffering.

There were times that were dark. She felt overwhelmed. But, even in those times, she cried out to God and sought comfort from our Heavenly Father. She sought wisdom. She sought courage. She sought strength. She worked long hours and still cared for Daddy selflessly. She prayed with him, she laughed with him, she slept by his side, and she often sang to him. Through his last years, she, too, saw his weakening and yet remained strong and vigilant.

On the morning of December 7th, I received a call from her best friend, urging me to come to my father's bedside. I knew that with the most recent stroke that he experienced a few weeks earlier that another one would not only be imminent, but probably take his life. I was right. By his side, sat his angel, his partner, his nurse, the love of his life – my stepmom. During his final hours, she recalled moments of joy and laughter. She made sound decisions and spoke clearly of what my Dad's wishes were. Regardless of how much this woman of God was hurting, her strength showed in all she did and said that day.

That same strength came back to her in his final moments before he went Home. She sang him his favorite gospel hymn, "What a Day That Will Be." The voice of an angel she had! She sang every word of that song, holding his hand as I sat on the other side of him, beckoning the Lord to bring Daddy home.

As I felt the most amazing feeling of peace in His presence, I heard not only the final chorus come to an end, I heard my Daddy's last breath. Hallelujah! His pain and suffering had ended! He was safely in the arms of Jesus and I was smiling at the Heavens as I said goodbye.

I learned so much in that very season. I learned that a woman of God is not made of steel; she cries. A woman of God does not wear a red cape and fight battles with superhuman strength; she leans into the arms of a mighty Warrior to protect her.

A woman of God does not sit idly by, quietly, and allow the world to dictate her next move; she is diligent, courageous and seeks God's will above her own. A woman of God does not make decisions on her own; she seeks the wisdom of the All Knowing and allows Him to steer her. Faithful and devoted, she makes her husband proud and her children praise her! Loving and merciful, her hands heal. However, *she* is not to be idolized, as she is simply a reflection of Jesus...**He** is to be worshiped because of her!

My Dad led a long, blessed life and it was not always a smooth ride. He hurt deep inside and may have made some bad choices, but who doesn't? He asked God to heal him. God asked me to pray over him and be by his side when he shared his deepest concerns. I listened. I reassured him of God's promises and knew in my heart that his time was near.

Upon that final moment, I became the most aware of God's desire for my life. The irrepressible joy that He wants me to have despite these dark moments. The inspiration that would motivate me to end this series so appropriately...to be amid a *true* Proverbs 31 Woman! My loving Sister in Christ, my friend, my confidant, my stepmother.

A Prayer for You, Mama...

May God heal your moments of darkness and loneliness with a stillness of His presence. May He fill your heart with abundant joy of times past and a greater hope for a future serving Him. May every memory be a sweet one and usher in a renewed spirit of God's love for you.

Mama may your beautiful smile light up the lives and rooms like Daddy's did when you share your gift of laughter with others! May love never to be far from your hand, peace not to be far from your heart and hope to guide your steps. Thank you for showing me what it means to love – to truly love – as Jesus loves.

The love that you showed Daddy is the closest example of the agape love that God has for each one of us. Thank you for showing me grace, gentleness, and kindness as a friend. I praise God that He allows me freedom to speak my mind around you, be honest and not worry that I will be judged. You have shown me the level of acceptance that a Mother should have for her children, despite whether she agrees.

Heavenly Lord, equip her with the words to continue to speak truth and light into the lives of her children and grandchildren. May they see You in all she does and says. Grant her provision and safety...fellowship within the body of Christ and guide her obedient service to You. Bless her abundantly, Lord. Love her and give her peace...

It is in Your Son's most beautiful Name I pray.

Amen.

With love and appreciation,
Sweetpea

FIRSTS

The Christmas carols were everywhere, but I didn't hear your voice singing them with your own lyrics. The New Year's horns were blown and although the lines were clear, I still waited for your call at midnight. Oh, my favorite, funny Valentine! Via Delarosa was the song you belted out in Spanish in 2009 for Easter, remember? I played the video again to hear your voice. You did sound like a frog a little, but that was okay. It was still beautiful.

Guess what? Brandon came home on my birthday and at 8:03 pm I looked at the phone again, hoping that it would ring. You always called on my birthday at the very time I was born. No one else does that or ever has since that last call you made...

Our funny girl, Shylah, went to Heaven alongside you to keep you company yet left me aching for just one more of her sweet puppy kisses on my cheek as I cried myself to sleep. Losing her like I did; only you would really understand the hole in my heart. Oh, how my heart hurt. I just prayed for the pain to stop. Did you hear me?

Friday morning, I woke to your memory again. I can close my eyes and see your smile – that same smile that could light up the room! I hear you clapping your hands yelling, "There she is, my baby!" and feel your safe embrace, hugging me like only a Daddy can! You never liked to call it your birthday; you preferred "My Special Day."

Well, I am sure that you would tell me that I am wasting my tears right now. That you are enjoying your "Special Day" in Heaven with Jesus!

But I am crying anyway; I miss you. Not just today, but every day. And as I hit these 'firsts' without you, I miss you even more.

I guess that "I'll see you then." Okay?

We can celebrate a whole new string of firsts together...in Heaven... without the tears.

I love you Daddy!
Your Sweetpea

A Glimpse...

So during this season of my life when I finally finished this series, I recall the rush of being married, sending my son to war, suddenly becoming a mom of a toddler! I began writing this when I was still single, celebrating my new life in Him, and feeling the tingling of the Holy Spirit for the first time! How did I go from a place of singleness and consuming growth to a season of activity and numerous changes? Moving, job changes, new cars, expanded family, and I was still reeling from losing my Dad.

How did I do it?

I prayed.

God walked me through the following revelations by giving me circumstances. Situations where my efforts were not enough. My thoughts were small. My great plans were short-sighted, and my resources were unreliable. Whether I was praying for deliverance from the resurfacing of past mistakes or petitioning God for a breakthrough, I was praying. In some cases, standing in the gap for someone close to me while they faced imminent danger or failing health. During those times, I also learned about fasting.

The complete and unyielding dependence on Him. Food, social media, TV, or anything that took me away from the very presence or ability to solely focus on Him was how He brought me familiar with this concept.

Although new to me, I learned what the sacrifice brought. I learned the obedience and the faith stretching it brought. I recall the renewal and renovation of my life it brought. Prayer changed everything for me. In some cases, it even changed things for others. Some knew; some didn't. Lives may have been spared, health issues, or other miracles may have been a result of my humbled position on my knees! I don't know. Maybe one day, I will know.

Maybe one day, Jesus Himself will show me the outcome of those prayers and the difference that they may have made to someone. The difference they made to me.

The difference it made to Him.

One day.

IN PURSUIT OF BECOMING

a Praying Woman

INTRODUCTION
Why Do I Pray?

As faithful servants of God, many of us have become more involved with Bible studies, small groups and ministry work. We need now, more than ever, to remain connected to Him through prayer! He has called you to follow Him and you have dedicated your heart to Him. Let's devote some time to study the dynamics of prayer and open up a clearer discernment of His will for not just our lives, but also for lives of the ones He brings closest to us!

Why do I pray? As I have become more aware of how important it is to nurture my relationship with God, I have become increasingly drawn to prayer. Not just during those times of meditation after reading His Word, but *all* the time. I yearn to remain in the presence of God and maintain a communion with Him that is unique to *our* relationship. I find that as I lean into Him for guidance in my life, I am also honoring Him in coming to Him in prayer.

The reverence of my prayer is not sprinkled with any ritual but involves just an honest surrender to His sovereign power. He is my Creator, and how can I move along the mundane of this world without first consulting in the One who gave me life? He has awakened me to feel His presence when I speak to Him and shown me how to trust Him with the innermost sinews of my heart. Reverence to His Majesty's company and honoring Him through prayer just comes naturally as I draw nearer to Him.

> *"Those persons who know the deep peace of God, the unfathomable peace that passes all understanding, are always men and women of much prayer."*
>
> **~ R.A. Torrey**

I depend on God and as I actively devote my heart to serving Him. I acknowledge that without Him, I may have some success, but it will only be temporary and lack any sustainable value. There is a state of helplessness that I feel without God. I wait for Him.

> *"Because of the LORD's great love we are not consumed, for His compassions never fail. They are new every morning; great is Your faithfulness. I say to myself,*
> *'The LORD is my portion; therefore I will wait for him.'*
> *The LORD is good to those whose hope is in Him, to the one who seeks Him; it is good to wait quietly for the salvation of the LORD."*
>
> **~ Lamentations 3:22-26**

I also see that prayer has brought to me the personal desires of my heart. Desires that God knows already and although not every one of my prayers were answered the way I wanted them to, He later showed me that as I came into alignment with His will, the desires of my heart changed anyway. I have learned that along with God redirecting my steps as He gently sometimes said no, He also faithfully brought me to something *much* better! He ultimately knows what is best for me.

God is consistent in His character and the heart of God is often revealed to His people when He answers our petitions…or when He doesn't. What is also consistent with God's character is that He may not always change my <u>circumstance</u>, but he may radically change me and give me the discernment, courage, and strength to change the circumstances **myself**.

Through consistent prayer, He has changed my viewpoint and enlightened me to His perspective. Seeing the same situation that I may be in prayer over through His eyes, changes my heart towards it and then His heart's desires become my own.

> "Take delight in the LORD, and he will give you the desires of your heart."
> ~ **Psalm 37:4**

Praying with sincerity and based on God's Word has forged me into this ever-evolving disciple that He is constantly at work in.

I know that many before me prayed: Jeremiah, Daniel, Moses, King David, Job, and so many more! They each petitioned God in a variety of ways, yet they set themselves apart to live a life that gave God glory. As I recall many of the ancient prophets and people of the Bible, I saw evidence of that same God that I spend time with every day.

The God of Jacob is my God! When I cry out to Him as Job did when his kingdom and family were torn from him, the same merciful God is listening! When I stand in the presence of God and witness

His glory as Moses did, I am positive that my face glows, as well! I ask God to hear my sincere aching and confessions – although He already knows them all. He beckons me to have a contrite heart, even in times of praise, to ensure that I have a heart that still stands in awe of His supreme governance in my life!

A heart of loving obedience...

> *"The sacrifices of God are a broken spirit;*
> *a broken and contrite heart, O God, you will*
> *not despise."*
>
> **~ Psalm 51:17**

Having described what I discovered to be the soundest reasons to pray, God lay on my heart, through a soft whisper, to dive into a new series. He asked me to study prayer. Not just *partake in* more of it (although that is never a bad idea), but to carefully and purposefully discover a few types of prayer. Among these types of prayer, we will be examining are prayers of Petition, Deliverance, Thanksgiving, Consecration/Purity, Intercession, and Supplication.

> *"Pray without ceasing."*
>
> **~ 1 Thessalonians 5:17**

Through these various forms of prayer, we will strive to better understand the character and heart of God during times past with the likes of prophets, kings, shepherds, disciples, and even Jesus Himself! We will position ourselves to be more receptive to God's prompting of our hearts. We will connect with Him through consistent and fervent prayer. Together, we will commit to sincere prayer, knowing that through it, we will have increased hope, stronger character, and, in some cases, restored faith.

I believe with all my heart that God is calling His people. And He is calling us at a rapid rate. I believe that He wishes to have every heart call out to Him with sincere and earnest yearning to abide in His presence before it is too late. God loves us, this we know. But to really, *really know* and experience the agape love of God begins with communion with Him. It begins by a non-legalistic cadence of conversation with the Holiest Host. It begins by asking God to examine our hearts and purify our minds. Praying opens the door to a personal and deeply fulfilling relationship with the One Who loves you and desires to not only have you near Him always, but also to hear your voice, beloved....

Will you journey with me?

Let's Pray

My glorious Lord! Each day, I bow my head and speak to you. I reveal to You the recesses of my heart and confess to You all the times I have fallen short, as if You don't already know. However, I know that Your desire is for me to voice to You my sins and concerns of my life. You have been so very faithful...so loving... so just...and consistent. Even through my wavering, You always take me back!

Hallelujah, God...my precious and loving Father! Thank You! Thank You for showing me how to communicate with You, develop our relationship, and nurture my space in Your heart! Whether it is through praying for someone else, requesting favor or mercy, crying out in pain, lifting my voice in praising You, or simply standing in awe of Your magnificence...Your presence is so strong! You have given me assurance that I rest in the palm of Your hand!

I pray, Holy God, that the women who wish to develop a more fulfilling relationship with You find that, through prayer, they will begin to feel Your presence among them. I pray that they do not let the enemy speak untruths into their minds by telling them that they are not equipped to pray or that somehow, You won't hear them!

I banish all and every principality of darkness and shadow of Hell that comes against the renewed relationship You will have with Your precious Daughters. In the Name of Christ Jesus, there will be no interruption, delay, distraction, doubt, fear, lie, or weakness that will stand in the threshold of their yearnings to be closer to You, Abba! Hallelujah, my Lord.

I love You, and so do the women reading this. Call to us to draw nearer and to feel Your touch. Hear the beautiful sound of Your

Daughter's voice as she greets her King through her whispered prayer! Guide us, Lord. In Your Son's most Holy Name I pray these things...

Amen.

PRAYERS OF PETITION

"Draw near to God and He will draw near to you."
      ~ **James 4:8**

*I*N THE GARDEN OF Gethsemane, Jesus Himself petitioned God for his own life. Although He was, above all else, the most obedient to God, He still requested that the events aligned by God's would be somehow changed to spare Him of the greatest suffering ever known. However, in His petition still came the acknowledgment of God's supremacy and sovereignty through the words,

> *"O My Father, if it is possible, let this cup pass from Me; nevertheless, not as I will, but as You will"*
>   ~ **Matthew 26:39**

God desires for us to bring to Him in prayer everything from our most basic need to the greatest anguish that we may be facing. Although His will be done in our lives, it is up to us to surrender to God and acknowledge that He truly <u>does know</u> what is best for us. He has positioned events to unfold that would not only align for His will for our lives, but also for His will among the lives of those we touch.

Sometimes, I have realized, that it goes beyond me during those times that I am most suffering and perhaps these events (or lessons) are part of the will for someone else altogether. Although I petition God to grant my desire and need, it may only be granted as it ties into the life of someone else. I may have to live a testimony through a fire to serve as a proponent of God's will overall.

> *"For you did not receive the spirit of bondage again to fear, but you received the Spirit of adoption by whom we cry out, 'Abba, Father.'"*
> **~ Romans 8:15**

It is not only His desire for us to ask for what we need, but it is through our heritage as adopted children of a Most High God that it is expected for us to come to Him as if we were heading towards the lap of our earthly Dads! How safe we feel there! No fear from the lies of the enemy, no harm from bondage; just safety and assurance that He hears us and beckons us to trust Him unequivocally.

> *"Oh come, let us worship and bow down; Let us kneel before the Lord our Maker. For He is our God, and we are the people of His pasture, And the sheep of His hand."*
> **~ Psalm 95:6-7**

So... *How*? How do we come to Him with a prayer asking for anything when the God of all Creation already knows all we need and may be in the process of granting our request anyway? Well, first, I am of the opinion that prayer is not something that requires a set posture, i.e. head down, eyes closed, knee bent, palms up, etc. Moses petitioned God standing up. Daniel prayed before he spoke to someone (and while he was speaking), Saul fell on his face, and Paul cried out in prison.

However, metaphorically speaking, each of these wise men bowed down before God! With abandon and surrender, they removed their pride, their prejudice, their self from the situation and pleaded to God for His will to be done – regardless of what they prayed for.

It takes humility before God to ask Him to grant you the desire of your heart and voice your limited ability to provide it for yourself. Leaning into His ability to place in motion the events to help unfold the results you ask for takes a faith; a strong one! A strong one that not only believes that the Lord will deliver but being satisfied with whatever He grants although it may come in a package far different from what we envision!

In petition, have faith that you are heard, you are delighted in, and He is already way ahead of you, Sister. Allow Him to hear you speak of your surrender and trust in Him. Still, know that without taking some time to focus on your needs, you may have a hard time discerning your priorities. That is what God will help you do... take your mind off of your immediate suffering, gain some much-needed clarity, and connect with Him on a more intimate level.

Through this connection, He may very well help you find the solutions yourself and give you the strength to act upon this new-found wisdom.

> *"The fear of the LORD is the beginning of wisdom; all who follow his precepts have good understanding.*
> *To him belongs eternal praise."*
>
> **~ Psalm 111:10**

Let's Pray

Lord, throughout our prayer lives, we are faced with times that aside from thanking You for all You have done, we ask of You for the deepest desires of our hearts. It could be from asking You to guide us through another long day at work, granting provision, or healing a loved one from an illness. No matter what the need or desire, we yearn to come to You in humble spirit and surrender in knowing Your sovereignty reigns in all situations.

We wish to have Your will be done not just in our lives, but also in the lives of the people surrounding us. We acknowledge that may mean that circumstances may not filter out the way that we hoped for, but we trust in You...trust that through the pain, confusion, despair, shock, or grief that You will bring favor and understanding to those who trust and believe in You...in Your time...in Your way!

Forgive us for the times of unbelief, the times of doubt and for when our pride or arrogance gets in the way, when we fall short... thank You for loving us, hearing us, and holding us close when we submit to You. You long to hear our voices cry out to You and admit our weakness and frailty without You. You do not wish for us to suffer; however, You wish to grant us the wisdom that comes from fearing You and seeking understanding and for those times where situations escape our understanding or acceptance.

Your reign in our lives is supreme. It is holy. It is pure and from it, brings us strength. Abba, we seek Your assistance, Your guidance, Your will. Light our steps and reveal to us what we seek the most...You. In the name of Your precious Son, Christ Jesus, we pray.

Amen.

THE PRISONER

Warmth of the rays dancing across the quilt as quiet giggles are heard in the next room...the lighting awaits as the darkness swallows the room...he doesn't see the shadows right away, they surface later – when he least expected them to. How can this be? How can anyone ever believe him? If he fights against them, then he might win, and no one will have to know.

Or will they figure it out?

The cell is closed, and the warden stifles the prisoner for another day; however, he sees the light under the door from his cell. Who is in there? Will they be able to talk the warden into letting him go? But what if this is a test? Perhaps it is a test that forbids his soul from wandering anymore? A test that finds his weakest point and uses it to strengthen someone else... A test...

But wait.

The sound of footsteps echo in the hallway and as the sound gets louder, the snickering begins. Stabbing into the stillness is a fear unlike any fear made by man. It penetrates the deepest sinews of his heart as he sees the past in the shadows and realizes the time has come to pay.

The howling cries of those who were in pain haunt him. He sees the wall. What does it say now? The words are unclear. The footsteps stop. The snickering stops.

The door opens and the light sears through the veil of grey like lightning. It's quick, and then it disappears! The light disappears!

Familiar scraping against metal is heard. He hears it and immediately recognizes it.

The cell is opened...then, silence...

Coolness replaces the stench and heat. The air is still. From a distance, it resembles peace. But how can it be? It's been this dark for so long and the echoes were his comfort. But what about the routines and the numbers on the floor... Who will carry on? The release of anguish seems too real.

Too real. It is all too real.

What will they say?

So the prisoner retreats to the cell corner, where it is darkest.

Familiar. Comfortable. Alone.

But the door remains open.

Seashells and sand pebbles on pink carpet are what he sees when he closes his eyes tonight. In his dreams, the sun doesn't set, the warmth of the quilt doesn't fade, and lightning doesn't await him. If only he could stay asleep because braving the unknown, he is not equipped for.

For now, he will sleep.

PRAYERS OF DELIVERANCE

"Be pleased, O LORD, to deliver me: O LORD, make haste to help me."
																	~ Psalm 40:13 (KJV)

There have been times in our lives where the fear of the unknown, the reality of a circumstance being unchangeable by our own means and imminent danger seem to overcome the very psyche of our souls! As I was in prayer for God to reveal to me what He wanted me to share, He had me look back to the life before I knew Christ.

If only I could remember all the times where I experienced an inability to discern the best avenue out of the situation I was in. I know that there were many times and many feelings of hopelessness and despair that rocked my very foundation. Before I committed my life to Christ, crying out to God in those desperate or confusing times seemed to be *the last thing* I did. By God's very grace and mercy did He deliver me each time regardless of my obedience or active faith. I rarely stopped long enough after the ordeal or season of time to thank *Him* for saving me – ***once again***!

I went through breakups, illness, loneliness, job loss, abandonment, and betrayal for many years picking up every self-help book I could find to give me a quick and easy fix to my issues. Searching for an outline for a ten-step "How To" that would guide me down the road of recovery and happiness... searching, searching...yet, I remained empty and lost. I did not even realize that during this whole time of *self-inflicted* pain and darkness, I lay vulnerable and subject to even more discontent.

> *"Be sober-minded; be watchful. Your adversary the devil prowls around like a roaring lion, seeking someone to devour."*
>
> **~ 1 Peter 5:8**

In this darkness, there were glimpses of light that appeared to me. People would mention to me that I was lost or just finding my way but I never knew what they meant. I didn't know enough about what they were talking about to even be offended, intrigued, or enlightened. I needed deliverance in my life, but I didn't know what lay on the other side of it. I didn't know what it would even look to find my way! Besides, how would I even begin? I saw people in love all around me, but I was alone. I saw people with long tenure with good companies, but I secretly loathed my job and was on the brink of losing it. I witnessed joy in others, but I struggled to have fun, even during a night out with my closest friends. Something was missing. Then I read this verse one day:

> *"Do not conform to the pattern of this world but be transformed by the renewing of your mind. Then you will be able to test and approve what God's will is—His good, pleasing and perfect will."*
>
> **~ Romans 12:2**

I was carrying a great deal of resentment, anger, frustration, and bitterness. I needed to truly break free from these things. I needed God's deliverance from the bondage that was holding me back from the joy that I knew was possible. After all, I saw others with it. They told me about finding my way, but this time I listened to the rest of what they had to say. I was to find my way...<u>to God</u>! I decided to truly be delivered from the chains that were holding me down.

I knew that I needed to radically change not only my heart, my lifestyle, and my belief system, but most importantly, my mind! I needed to ensure that whatever finding my way meant, that it included a sustainable path that I would follow; however, unlike anything found inside of any self-help book, I had to really work for this. I had to begin by humbly putting myself before God! Earnestly, I cried out to God, like David did as he was being pursued by King Saul:

> *"Have mercy on me, my God, have mercy on me, for in you I take refuge. I will take refuge in the shadow of your wings until the disaster has passed. I cry out to God Most High, to God, who vindicates me. He sends from heaven and saves me, rebuking those who hotly pursue me, God sends forth His love and His faithfulness."*
> ~ **Psalm 57:1-3**

Praise God! He heard my prayers! Like in the beginning of **John 15:7 (NKJV)**, *"If you abide in Me, and My words abide in you."* I knew that I needed to lodge myself in Him and this would bind His healing to every area of my life! Like a prayer of petition, I was asking God for something. But not just for a new job, a cure from an illness, or forgiveness from a broken relationship – I was asking God to DELIVER me from the ways of life, of thought, of heart that led me to the brokenness! I was His and He yearned for me to prosper, to love, to be loved, to feel acceptance, to grow, to nurture, and serve others! He saved me from not only the snare of the evil one who comes to steal, kill, and destroy (**John 10:10**), but he saved me from myself!

Sisters, praying a prayer of deliverance is not just for the unsaved. Deliverance from bondage can happen at any time during your Christian walk. You, dedicated and focused to follow and serve our God, become a formidable force among the world. You shed light and grace into the darkness that has become so pervasive in our world. You cast out doubt and anxiety as others lose hope. You encourage during times of uncertainty.

This makes you a walking target for the enemy. Unless there has been ongoing consecration of mind and heart through obedience and undergirding of the Holy Spirit on a consistent basis, we lay vulnerable to the snares. With the same power that God used to raise Jesus from the grave, we must arm ourselves with this power, as a weapon against the enemy.

The most effective weapon in our arsenal is prayer! We must remain vigilant to His Word and pray for:

- Absence of fear
- Revoking of demonic forces
- Hedges of protection
- Vacating of unholy thoughts
- Banishment of darkness covenants
- Breaking of generational curses
- Healing of diseases
- Releasing inner vows that are contrary to God's word

And the list goes on!

> *"The weapons we fight with are not the weapons of the world. On the contrary, they have divine power to demolish strongholds. We demolish arguments and every pretension that sets itself up against the knowledge of God, and we take captive every thought to make it obedient to Christ."*
>
> **~ 2 Corinthians 10:4-5**

And as I mentioned earlier, I used to forget the most important aspect of prayer. I used to forget to *thank* Him. Earnestly and whole-heartedly thank Him for His faithfulness and deliverance from the strongholds in my life; from the danger I was in or the passing of a disaster or trial I was facing.

Take note of Moses, praising God for His deliverance, His protection and His destroying of the enemies pursuing His people as they fled from Egypt. Moses and the people sang in **Exodus 15:1-18**, calling God "exalted, strength, defense, salvation, warrior, and awesome in glory." Our Holy God is all these things and so much more! Hallelujah!

Do not fear, do not be discouraged, and do not allow the enemy to take up residence in your life for any length of time! Ask upon God to deliver you, to deliver a loved one, a friend, or even an enemy in a time of disaster. As Moses and the people of Israel witnessed the parting of the Red Sea, you will witness the working of God's arm of justice in your life.

Building your faith, this will further equip you to minister to others during times of needed deliverance. As well, our confidence and faith in His sovereignty will manifest in our lives as strength in spirit. Spirit indwelled with the mightiness that will cast down these strongholds, freeing us from the chains that bind us and separate us from the presence of God.

Let's Pray

My Holy God! How You have delivered not only me, but those that I love from the snare of the enemy! How You have manifested a protection so impenetrable that those around me stand in awe as we witness the omnipotence of Your hand over the situations and people we lift to You.

Your faithful promises are true. You have stood in the gap of my unbelief and given me the testimony today to share with those who are yearning to gaze upon Your face. We take authority over the principalities and powers of the darkness that come against the Truth of Your Word; binding them up and casting them into the pit of Hates where they belong!

We speak against the strongholds of generational curses that have plagued our families for so long. Bitterness, poverty, anger, unforgiveness, manipulation, and strife are not of You...may we have You search us for these things and remove them from us! Consecrate our hearts, Lord – purify our souls – transform our minds! May all that we know, we feel, we hear, we see, we speak, or what we yearn for be only from the beauty and purity of Your creation.

From the darkness of the world, may we stand out and be regarded as Your saints, bringing light into those dim places. May we walk with You, Abba, and confidently stand firm on the foundation of Your Word as we fight against the very things that attempt to destroy us? The battles have been waged but the war has already been won!

Our Mighty King is victorious and as we are credited with the righteousness found in Christ, we are equally triumphant in anything that we claim in the name of Christ! To the glory of our Father, may all the things we petition earnestly before You, God, manifest! In the matchless name of Christ Jesus, we pray.

Amen!

PRAYERS OF INTERCESSION

*"Oh, that one might plead for a man with God,
as a man pleadeth for his neighbor!"*
~ Job 16:21

"**P**LEASE PRAY FOR ME!" I hear that often. I say it often. I've been part of intercessory prayer for as long as I have been a Christian. But, as I stop and think about what it truly signifies within the body of Christ, I become more aware of how powerful this type of prayer truly is.

Begin with the concept of intercession being not only a petition to our Most Holy God, but also a sacred communication on behalf of another. I used the word *sacred* because, as in earnest prayer, we must have reverence to Whom we petition, belief in Him to fulfill those requests in accordance to His will, and a faith to remove ourselves from the situation, relying not on words, but the abundant Spirit of God to voice, on our behalf, the desires of our hearts. A fully-devoted and conscience quietening of mind to communion with God during a time of need is what, in my opinion, depicts the stillness that God will often use to speak directly to us.

God has revealed to me that I am not above anyone else or without blemish myself, so as I am coming before Him to stand in the gap for someone else's requests, I must begin by acknowledging that I am as dependent on Him for my own strength and humbly deny my *own* opinion; allowing Him to fully use me for His glory in the situation. I must be fervent in my prayer; confessing faith in His sovereignty over the situation and reliance on His way being above mine!

> *"'For my thoughts are not your thoughts,*
> *neither are your ways my ways,' declares the*
> *Lord. 'As the heavens are higher than the earth,*
> *so are my ways higher than your ways and my*
> *thoughts than your thoughts.'"*
>
> **~ Isaiah 55:8-9**

He has shown me that a repentant heart is an ongoing attribute of a conscience Christian, but especially during prayer is He most interested in hearing our profession of faith and confession of heart! We must be of the understanding that this is something that God requires from us, regardless of petition or situation. Also, in this same state of heart, as an intercessor, I willingly take on the burden of the petitioner as I stand in agreement with them in prayer.

As Nehemiah prayed for the people of Israel, he did not set himself apart from the people, but instead lamented with the same grievous heart to God. He earnestly shared the emotion and urgency of the people for immediate deliverance.

> *"When I heard these things, I sat down and wept. For some days I mourned and fasted and prayed before the God of heaven. Then I said: 'Lord, the God of heaven, the great and awesome God, who keeps his covenant of love with those who love him and keep his commandments, let your ear be attentive and your eyes open to hear the prayer your servant is praying before you day and night for your servants, the people of Israel. I confess the sins we Israelites, including myself and my father's family, have committed against you. We have acted very wickedly toward you. We have not obeyed the commands, decrees and laws you gave your servant Moses."*
>
> ~ **Nehemiah 1:4-7**

Another purpose of intercessory prayer that God revealed to me was the opportunity we are given to actively witness to someone. Imagine if the person who cries out to you, "Pray for me," does not have a strong faith. If you are yielding to the Holy Spirit and allowing Him to help you discern this, He will guide your words to minister directly to the heart of another!

This type of self-discipline in your servanthood will surely be acknowledged and blessed by God, Sister! Can you imagine (or maybe you have already experienced this) having that small window of opportunity to speak words of hope into some one's life when they are humbly asking for prayer?

Perhaps, the fact that they are asking for prayer may be a first step to their accepting Christ? Patience during this moment is not only a sweet fruit of the Spirit, but a critical component of surrendering self to the Spirit and *truly listening* to the person. I can admit that earlier in my Christianity I anticipated too much of someone's acceptance of Christ and I missed the opportunity to install hope and self-testimony to further assist the decision to follow Jesus. Not only within myself must I show patience, but also encourage the person to have patience with their faith.

Establish that pervasive truth that His timing is what governs the situation, *not ours*. Remind the person during this time that God does reveal more and more of Himself to us as we lean into Him; trusting Him to teach us valuable lessons throughout our wait.

> *"Yet those who wait for the LORD Will gain new strength. They will mount up with wings like eagles, they will run and not get tired, they will walk and not become weary."*
> **~ Isaiah 40:31**

Earnestly and faithfully seeking the will of God as we pray for others in their situation is not only a duty of a professed Christian, but in my opinion, a privilege that I do not ever intend of taking for granted. As I stand in the gap for others, I know that there will be an opportunity for someone to stand in the gap for me when the time comes as I have already I have experienced on many occasions, intercessory prayer concerning family issues, health concerns, comfort during a trial or even for clarity of direction.

I have been rewarded an overwhelming peace in knowing that I have true prayer warriors that have been appointed to me by God in those times! I have witnessed miracles as a result. I have experienced healing; both mine and others. I have grown in the Lord and watched others grow as a result. I have stood amazed as God answers the most intimate of prayers; both mine and others.

My personal story, alone, is a testament to intercessory prayer! Whether it was a friend in Christ or a praying Momma on her face before God on my behalf, I can confidently say that prayer has changed the most seemingly unchangeable circumstance and the most seemingly unchangeable heart.

> *"Is anyone among you sick? Let them call the elders of the church to pray over them and anoint them with oil in the name of the Lord. And the prayer offered in faith will make the sick person well; the Lord will raise them up. If they have sinned, they will be forgiven. Therefore, confess your sins to each other and pray for each other so that you may be healed. The prayer of a righteous person is powerful and effective."*
>
> **~ James 5:14-16**

Persistence before the Cross allows us to selflessly become part of a greater purpose. A purpose to further *His* Kingdom through *His* will and in *His* timing. It doesn't force God to change His mind on anything. He doesn't change His mind about anything anyway. He simply and consistently ordains the way in which His will is done. To be part of that process is a true blessing and miracle of God! Like Moses' pleading with the Lord in Exodus 32 not to destroy the people, he did not change God's mind about it, he simply molded his own heart to the desires of God by standing up for the very people that he was appointed to lead! He stood confidently in the gap for the lost of that nation, eventually leading them forward and showing them God's mercy first hand.

One final thought...when we engage in intercessory prayer, we choose to pray as Jesus did. He was the most effective Intercessor of all time. On our behalf, He reconciled us to our Heavenly Father. He burdened Himself with our sin and our petitions to God to become of pure souls, *permanently*. He healed. He calmed and comforted. He performed miracles. He walked among men of all types and faced the greatest persecution in history.

However, He *never ceased* praying. Not only on His own behalf in the Garden of Gethsemane before His crucifixion, but even in His final moments before His death, hanging on the cross, He forgave one of the thieves! And He has never stopped interceding for mankind. To this day (even right now), He continues to intercede to the Father on your behalf, Sister.

We yearn to be more like Him, right? Then intercessory prayer is part of your DNA as a Christian. Allow the Holy Spirit to guide you as you stand in the gap for someone today. Listen and watch for the opportunity to witness, to comfort, to heal, to bless, and to stand beside a child of God as they humbly ask you, "Please pray for me!"

Let's Pray

My gracious and loving God, I come before You today in hopes of pleasing Your heart! I ask, Lord to continue to guide me in Your will. Allow me to stand in the gap for Your people. Equip me with the wisdom to speak Your Truth and Light into the lives of those reading this today.

May Your healing power indwell within their minds and embark them on a journey to boldly pray for others more often. May we all be sensitive to the presence of the Spirit as we yield to His prompting for us to speak over others during their times of need. May we be humbled by the appointment of our mouths and hands to speak and touch the lives of the ones who are seeking, Abba. They seek Your guidance, Your mercy, Your strength, Your healing, Your comfort, Your light in their lives.

Grant us the discernment to know when to speak. Your Word guards our speech and provides us with the guidance to use It during times of witnessing. It is not by our own strength or knowledge, but it is by Your Spirit that we walk with those who are pressing in, curious to the Way that they have heard of.

Father touch our hearts to remain humble, repentant, and contrite as we come before You during prayer. Above all, allow us the appointed time to share our testimony of Your faithfulness. Pour favor into the lives of those who pray for others fervently and with earnest obedience. May their seats beside Your throne be adorned with the most precious of gold and stones of color.

Thank You, God for those who devote time on their faces before You in petition for others. Their selfless service to Your people reflect the unyielding love Your Son has for us! May we all arrive to the place where Your love is reflected in all we do. Have mercy upon us when we place our needs above others...it is Your grace that sustains us for all our days.

As You call Your people, Abba, allow us who have chosen to believe in Your great Name, be appointed the opportunity to lead the lost to You. Your will be done, Lord. It is through the Holy Spirit in the matchless and beautiful Name of Your Son, Christ Jesus, I pray all these things.

Amen.

A Glimpse...

Just before I met my husband, I participated in a Purity Ceremony with a good friend of mine at the time; we were prayed over by a group of pastors at my home church and made a vow before the Lord to remain celibate until we married our future husbands. This part of my testimony is probably the one most painful because, although I did not fall victim in my life to any sexual molestation or abuse, I was exposed to sexuality at a very early age. From masturbation, bi-sexuality, to promiscuity and a hedonistic lifestyle throughout my life, the Lord met me in this dark place one day and challenged me to embark on a journey away from this place forever. He knew that my bags would take a while to pack, I would stumble and spend a lifetime being delivered from such egregious idolatry.

Among the early exposure to sexual sin, was the front row seat to witnessing members of my family sin with reckless abandon! Drugs, pornography, alcohol, and even the occult. There was no stone unturned! I processed such debauchery and immoral behavior as normal. By the time I was 20, I was pregnant out of wedlock with my son. A short-lived marriage was followed by five years of sexual and immoral sin above and beyond what I saw when I was younger. Another marriage followed. Another divorce right after it. More sin. More darkness. More bondage.

The path was a long one. It was filled with story after story of married men, near death experiences, and dabble in the occult. Sexual sin was my normal and I used my sexuality as a weapon to get what I wanted.

And it worked.

Until Jesus met me right where I was and showed me who I was to become.

PRAYERS OF CONSECRATION AND PURITY:
A Personal Testimony

*"Create in me a pure heart, O God,
and renew a steadfast spirit within me."*

~ Psalm 51:10

THE PRODDING OF THE Holy Spirit is powerful! I pondered for months on how to approach the subject of purity from a standpoint that would not come across as self-righteous or at all condemning. After all, that is not my heart and to remain obedient to Him is my desire above all else. He has directed me through this piece with a simple word: commitment.

Before we examine the ideal of commitment, may we side journey to the word 'consecration' first? When I think of the *act* of consecration, my mind immediately goes back to the Old Testament and the sprinkling of sacrificial blood at the Temple. I also think of the ritualistic cleansing that the priests would undertake – diligent and reverent to a most Holy and Omniscient God. To be undone amid His presence, to be destroyed and banished to hell if not found wholly pure must have been such a powerful and all-consuming fear!

Remember how they used to tie ropes around the waists of those who would enter the Temple, just in case they were found to be unclean? That way they could pull out their bodies once they were stricken down by God. Can you imagine for a moment what that scene looked like? Can you imagine what would go through your mind as you were called to step in next?

Praise our King, Jesus Christ for allowing us all to be consecrated in His spilled blood! His horrific crucifixion becomes a physical recognition of all our fallen and sinful selves being hauled out of sin by the waists! Thank You, Lord!

But praying for the consecrated life or the consecrated heart takes a level of serious commitment. Imagine requesting from God to gird you with a powerful discernment to avoid evil, evil doers, improper speech or deeds, or alignment with His decrees and then *willfully* entering the **very** places and situations that produce such things you have asked to be protected from! How does that make sense? I struggled with this for a couple of years after I rededicated myself to Christ. Being in the wrong places with an attitude of self-sufficiency or empowerment led me to a life of emptiness. I made steps to avoid a legalistic life, but internally struggled with what I was *supposed to* be doing.

I soon realized that it was the lead of the Holy Spirit that changed my actions to become more holy and stop putting myself into a position of question from not just those who are appointed to me during my Christian walk and will hold me accountable but, more importantly, to those who were watching my transformation first hand! My family and friends! How was I to speak of what Christ has done in my life yet continue to willingly place myself into those areas of targeted temptation?

How could I provide an effective witness to those who came to me seeking 'what was different' and offer them a clouded version of my salvation?

I knew in my deepest soul that I needed to lay down my heart, my soul, my mind, <u>and my body</u> before Christ to search me thoroughly for anything that was unclean.

Did I have to do this often? *Yes.*

To associate more completely with the Holy Spirit and participate in that sacred covenant with the Lord, there were some decisions that were warranted. I had to examine the people, places and things in my life. I had to review if any of these elements brought forth glory to God. And if they didn't, well, they were *removed*. Don't mistake what I am saying here. **I** didn't remove them. <u>God did</u>. I truly asked Him to step in and break strongholds of oppressive people, places, habits, speech, and thinking. Being the good Father that He is, He manifested situations that purged from my life (in some cases overnight) what was not of Him!

Setting me and my life apart from what was harmful to not only me at the time, but also harmful to what was to later come into my life was a necessary step. And sometimes a very painful one. I feel led to temper any further commentary with this statement.

> *God did not isolate me. He did not and does not call for abandonment, dissension, or disconnection to follow Him. He does not permit a volitional tearing away of His people from their families or people in their lives. Christianity and a fellowship/relationship with God are not a cult. I do not subscribe to the attitude of those who have mocked me or my faith as being anything more than a fear-based disposition*

> *fueled by ignorance of God's truth. Jesus' commands remain to love your enemies and love one another. Remember? Just because God decided to purge people from my life during a season, doesn't mean that I stopped loving them. I just know that as God is busily orchestrating all events for His will and purpose, that I must trust Him to reveal to me and to them His sovereignty. Dying to self has taken, at times, all my energy. But it is through Christ that I am sustained and recharged.*

During my rededicating, in efforts to recreate my inner world, the Holy Spirit pressed upon my heart one monumental decision that, even to this very day, I am shocked that I made. I was in the throes of change and my surroundings were changing. My friendships were changing. My thoughts and perceptions about things were changing. As I leaned in more to God, the less some areas of my life had appeal. One area of my life was my attitude towards sex. Yes, actual *sex*.

Without the gory details of my personal struggles in this area, I can openly admit to you that my attitude towards sex began when I was very young. As I matured (and I use *that term* loosely), I misinterpreted the whole concept of sex and sexuality to control outcomes and people (men or women) around me. It was not until I became much savvier in the world's usage of the same concept that I used my sexuality as a weapon, gravitating towards the wielding power it had to manipulate situations in my favor.

I knew in my heart that this was somehow twisted and that it would catch up to me sometime in the far future, but little did I realize how profound a transformation it would be!

I was reading in the New Testament, in the book of Colossians one day and came across the following Scripture:

> *"Since, then, you have been raised with Christ, set your hearts on things above, where Christ is, seated at the right hand of God. Set your minds on things above, not on earthly things. For you died, and your life is now hidden with Christ in God. When Christ, who is your life, appears, then you also will appear with him in glory. Put to death, therefore, whatever belongs to your earthly nature: sexual immorality, impurity, lust, evil desires and greed, which is idolatry. Because of these, the wrath of God is coming. You used to walk in these ways, in the life you once lived."*
> **~ Colossians 3:1-7**

I was stunned. Could the one area of my life that I was so accustomed to hiding in shame be suddenly out in the brightest of lights before my Creator? Perhaps. Could the Most High actually be speaking to *me* right at that moment? Perhaps. I quickly went to the back of my Bible and in the Concordance looked up the word sexuality. Wow! That led me all the way back to the Old Testament and throughout the Bible. Hours had passed and as I brought my mini-study to a close, tears streaming down my face as I met God within these holy pages, I landed here:

> *"It is God's will that you should be sanctified: that you should avoid sexual immorality; that each of you should learn to control your own*

> *body in a way that is holy and honorable, not in passionate lust like the pagans, who do not know God."*
>
> ~ ***1 Thessalonians 4:3-5***

The reality of this verse and the dozens of verses before it came crashing down on me so hard that I fell to my knees! I was in the middle of my living room physically but was seated at a place of repentance in the presence of God. I asked Him what was it that He needed me to do? How could this sinner's past be not only **forgiven** but in some way be **used** for good of His Kingdom? He essentially told me that I would need to give this yoke of bondage <u>to Him</u> and that He will work out the details with me later.

One of the details He had in mind was for me to tell my story as it relates to purity, progressive consecration, and biblical sanctification. Amazing, isn't it?

I met with a pastor, whom I love and respect very much, and asked him how do I go about making this pledge of purity. He counseled me thoroughly. He told me that making a solemn vow to God was not to be taken lightly and that I needed to be bathed in prayer in the days/hours leading to my formal vow and afterwards as Satan would take notice...and was he right!

See, I had met my future husband only months before this decision but we were not formally dating yet. As my old nature and Satan dictated lies to me, I wondered how was I going to capture this man's attention (or heart) if I didn't flaunt myself before him?

When I posed this same question to God in prayer, He promptly reminded me that He was enough for me – that God was ENOUGH for me – and if I didn't feel that way, then I had missed His will for me. Wow! Humbled, I said, *"Ok, Lord. You are enough for me. Allow*

Your will to be done in my life...for Your glory." And it was done. My angst and worry that I might be alone forever was instantly gone. Solid peace overwhelmed me like never before.

The church I attend held a private ceremony for me where the entire pastoral staff and their wives prayed over me. They stood in the gap for me as I made this covenant to remain celibate until marriage. I asked the Lord to help me to become whole again. I asked Him to help me remain in Him, to release emptiness, and guide me in my walk to becoming more of the Godly woman He had designed me to be. Help me to abstain, remain free from anything that would pollute my mind, spirit, or heart. Rid me of the guilt, shame, and evil that had tormented me for years in my sexuality.

This commitment was substantial. Those people who knew (the old) me thought that I had finally snapped and were worried. My own son, although hesitant and shocked, encouraged me to remain faithful and I vaguely remember him wishing me luck, but when I disclosed this to my future husband, who at the time was only a friend, his face beamed! He was intrigued and related to my past in this area as well. Soon, he was making this same vow in prayer to God.

A year and a half later, God honored our commitment by allowing us to join in matrimony...in **Holy** matrimony, just as He intended.

I'll end this segment by mentioning that consecration and purity are not just instantaneous rituals or decisions that are made because of reverence and obedience, but they are commitments that last a lifetime with God. I, by far, am not perfect. I struggle daily with sin and request for His forgiveness as I fall short. My commitment to God in this area of sanctifying my life – *all areas of my life* – and purifying my mind, heart, soul, and spirit- is a *daily* process. As I lean into His Word and will for His Kingdom, my purpose becomes clearer. As that purpose becomes clearer, it commands even more of a focus and diligent effort to take inventory of my life on a consistent basis to ensure that I am allowing God to reveal to me the things He needs me to rid of.

It hurts sometimes to recognize how broken I have been, but as God sees it, I am **beautifully broken** and just as He committed to me years ago that fateful date in my living room, He is still working out the details.

Thank You, Father!

Let's Pray

It is with the humblest and most broken heart today, Lord that I come to You. Although Your glory has been revealed today in our story, I feel heavy hearted for those who still may be feeling oppression in this area of their lives and only through Your Spirit and commitment to loving us, can this be revealed.

Lord, I have asked You to guide me through this testimony of Your great work of redemption and restoration in such a way that gives You glory and in no way condemns anyone who is reading it! I pray against any spirit of condemnation, oppression or guilt in Jesus' Name! I pray for a yearning to be established in the reader to bring before You their deepest places to have You shed light on the darkness that may still be lingering... Heavenly Father reveal to Your faithful servants those pieces of their lives that may need healing as it relates to consecration and purity of mind, spirit, soul and heart.

Help us all to remember our right-standing with You – as Your Word dictates to us! Our sainthood, our holiness, our inheritance, our friendship with Your Son, Christ Jesus, our embodiment of Spirit that dwells within us...assist and guide us to a place of boldness that we can revisit boundaries with friends/family and ensure that our relationships are pure, honest, and brought into the alignment of Your will.

Allow us, Abba, to become a beam of light to those around us, dispelling hypocrisy in our lives, setting examples for our children, our family, Your church. Forgive us when we fall short – we know You will never forsake us and will love us abundantly. Your Word says that You will provide us our needs according to Your glorious riches, those same riches that strengthen us through power of Your Spirit!

Your Son, Christ Jesus, paid the ultimate penalty for our sins and therefore consecrates us through His shed blood on Calvary that glorious day. There will be no power in this world that will ever separate us from this consecration and I ask, Father, for there to be a constant flow of awareness to those reading this right now of Your Majesty's strength in our lives to overcome temptation! The enemy stands alert to those who are single, going through marriage issues, and to those alone...he preys upon their minds, filling them with illusions of succumbing to unholy pleasures to fulfill imaginary voids. The only void that is real, Dear Lord, is the void in which You are not present!

You – not man, not pleasure, not sin, not self-gratification, not adultery, not idolatry – are missing! May there be a revival of surrender to You in every area of every life and may all shame and guilt be cast into the fiery pits of Hates as these things come to light. May all thoughts and actions be brought into the obedience of Christ. End the suffering of loneliness; replacing it with fellowship. End the suffering of addictions; replacing it with freedom and tangible fulfillment in Christ. End the allure of sexual perversions, discriminating acts of fornication, adultery; replacing it with that which is holy, pure, good, loving, righteous, and respectful. Free us from all that has oppressed us or has kept us from living in the fullness of You!

As we line up our lives to Your great will, You have promised us the desires of our hearts... Your Word never returns void! We have faith in a Most High God, a most loving Father to deliver us from darkness into a pure and sanctified life that reflects Your infinite love!

We praise You, we adore You and ask all these things in the Name that sets above all names, Jesus Christ.

Amen Selah.

PRAYERS OF THANKSGIVING AND SUPPLICATION

"Be anxious for nothing, but in everything by prayer and supplication, with thanksgiving, let your requests be made known to God."

~ Phil. 4:6

When concluding any series of writings, I always petition the Lord to show me a way to express to my readers the passion that resonates from His revelation to me while summarizing everything that He has shown me. For the last several months, He has been working within my life to give me clarity in this area and provide the next steps for my Ministry! Praise God!

Additionally, throughout this series, He has enlightened me to the various ways to communicate to Him through prayer and how to boldly come before Him with my heart. Ushering in His presence through prayer is a way to keep closer connection with Him, but recently He has been showing me that it is through *praise* and *thanksgiving* in my prayer time that He steps in closer!

> "But You are holy,
> Enthroned in the praises of Israel."
>
> **~ Psalm 22:3**

How God confirms for each of us His presence is as unique as His relationship with you, Sister. For me, I feel goose bumps and emotionally I feel lighthearted *(I have been known sometimes to even giggle when He steps close to me…the joy is overwhelming!)*. In my mind, a sound peace overtakes it and rushing thoughts of deadlines, chores, issues with family, finances, etc. all disappear! I become very aware that it is just me and just Him…

If I take this time to petition Him for a laundry list of things and then just simply stop, say Amen, and keep going…He hears me. If I take this time to cry out to Him and request safety or protection, stop and say Amen…He hears me. If I take this time to intercede for someone else – carefully listing their spoken requests for His care and mercy, stop, and say Amen…He hears me. Either way, He hears me. Well, in my prayer time, I have also added a series of Thank You's for the many things He has done in my life and for Who He is! I shift from the focus on <u>my need</u> to the focus on *His* sovereignty, *His* mercy, *His* grace, *His* love, *His* protection, *His* power, *His* clarity, *His* wisdom.

The whole dynamic of my time with Him changes! I hear my own voice rejoicing in His promises and reminding my heart of the **bigger** laundry list of <u>God's</u> countless acts of faithfulness!

"Praise the Lord! Oh give thanks to the Lord,
for He is good;
For His lovingkindness is everlasting."
~ Psalm 106:1

Examining this Scripture above, we are reminded to praise Him! Regardless of Bible versions available, any concordance is stock **full** of verses that reference the word "praise" *(Go ahead, look for yourself!).* In **Exodus 15: 1-18**, Moses is singing praises to God for His deliverance from Pharaoh's army and for God's mighty power and protection! In the book of Judges, Chapter 5, Deborah sings praises as well! She and Barak recall the strength and justice of the Lord.

From the book of Kings, to 1 Peter, and landing in the book of Revelation (**7:12**), *"Amen! Praise and glory and wisdom and thanks and honor and power and strength be to our God for ever and ever. Amen!"* In this we see the act of praising God runs parallel with recall His faithfulness, Sister! Does that point resonate with you?

Psalm 106:1 additionally reminds us to give thanks for the simple fact that God is GOOD! Yes, He is a God of power, of justice, of righteous wrath, of strength; an empowering life source of armies, devoted men and women of faith! But He is also GOOD! His loving kindness is evident all around us! His tender touch may come in a small whisper of a child, a beautiful sunset, a cloud overhead that is shaped like a rose, a cool breeze just when one more degree lift in the room would surely make you explode!

It could also be an answered prayer for healing, a long-awaited hug from a wayward child who has finally come home, a relief from a financial burden, and a recommitment from a husband who has been contemplating divorce. His kindness not only responds to your immediate physical needs, but sometimes, more importantly, to your deep-hearted ones. The needs that cause your soul to groan in such a way that only the Holy Spirit can interpret (**Romans 8:26**). And it's everlasting! He won't forsake you or turn His ear from your call.

> *"Hear my prayer, O Lord, Give ear to my supplications! Answer me in Your faithfulness, in Your righteousness!"*
>
> *~ Psalm 143:1*

Lastly, the word supplication may not be an everyday word for most people, so by definition, let's examine what this word means in context. Basically, it means to plead for something from a humble position, so if we are to present our prayers to God with confidence and grace (**Hebrews 4:16**), we are also to remain *humble*. Remember, Sisters, the Lord detests the proud, so being confident in His presence has more to do with our right-standing with Him and our sanctification than it does individual pride! Pride has no place before our God.

When we come to God with a pure heart and one of contriteness, we are professing our dependence on Him. We are leaving the pride we all feel when we are betrayed or witness an injustice to our family! We are not seeking God's vengeance on those issues or on the people that hurt us, instead we are pouring out our sincere and deepest pain. He hears that!

He reaches down – the Omniscient and Holy One – reaches down from Heaven and comforts you! In His faithfulness, He does not forsake or leave you lying there in your own misery. He already knows of your struggles today and is standing in TOMORROW, my friend! It is the simple fact that you have brought before God an earnest plea for the very things that He is already intimately aware of that delights His heart!

> *"Those who know your name trust in you, for you, Lord, have never forsaken those who seek you."*
>
> **~ Psalm 9:10**

In closing, throughout the Bible, where a powerful movement or even a subtle shift in attitude or event is celebrated, exaltation towards God include mention of His infinite sovereignty over the earth, His glorious creations among the land and the heavens, His assurance of promises kept, His agape love, His unswerving mercy, His peace, His protection, His deliverance, His glory, His strength, His power, His gentleness.

The list goes on and on. The stories of the Bible are timeless. They surpass boundaries we foolishly set in place in our minds. The people of the Bible seem to set the stage for generations of sin and selfishness. Some also show us what a true broken heart and sincere yearning to stand in the presence of God looks like. There are heroes like King David, Joshua, Joseph and Peter who sacrifice their families, their pride, and their lives for a touch of Heaven in their souls! They have sought after a Holy God and His will for not only their lives, but for the lives of their people with sobering passion and surrender!

Sisters, the modern world would have us deny God and His great works in exchange for an explanation that would satisfy our finite minds and our itching ears. The world would want us to place the God of the Universe in a nifty box to pull down from a spiritual shelf when we needed His power, grace, mercy or healing. Call upon Him when there is terror striking our land, our families, our rights! Beg for His angels when we are heading into oncoming traffic, then encourage anger towards Him when He doesn't deliver us in time!

However, when a child of God seeks His face, craves to be close to Him and know Him intimately, the taste of what the world serves us is bitter and frankly, sickening. We lift up our hands to Him for Who He is and for what He has accomplished through the greatest sacrifice for all mankind. We walk in the righteousness of being heir to the Kingdom of God. We lift our voices and hearts to the Heavens and shout out our praise to the One who removed generations of sin and despair from our future!

Whether we are petitioning Him for a new job, healing, interceding on a loved one's behalf, requesting consecration of spirit or deliverance from an abusive relationship, we must honor Him with PRAISE! We must call upon not only concrete examples of His faithfulness in our lives, but also the scores of "water-parting" events within our lineage! All these things in the past and what He has still left to accomplish in the future shows He is worthy of our praise!

Thank Him today, Sisters. With humble and open hearts, thank Him.

Let's Pray

Abba, today we lift our hearts and hands to You! We know of Your great sacrifice for our lives and the lives of our families. We know of Your great works – magnificent in wonder! We gaze upon Your creation and see all that reflects You! We have lived through times of trial and persecution so intense that we did not know if You were here. Forgive us Father, forever doubting that you left our side. We have been convinced that men abandoning us have left us as unworthy of love.

By Your truth and grace, we now understand that the Greatest of Men never did leave us and that through those times of loneliness, You were by our sides, embracing us. Numerous prayers, both big and small, have been answered and because of our own pride and self-absorption, we are not aware of Your presence and granting of us favor. We did not notice. May we turn from our own understanding and ways.

Your Word says that if we do walk from our evil ways and seek You, You will answer. O' God of my heart, hear the cries and moans of the hearts of those who just now see how they have been disconnected. May they feel the welcoming warmth of Your loving embrace! May they have etched in their hearts and minds this moment in time forever and always possess a yearning to feel this again. And again...and again!

But as You forge and fortify us with Your grace, may we also not just seek the feelings of the past with You, but instead search out new experiences, new anointing and fresh revelations of Spirit each time that we are seated in Your presence!

Thank You for hearing our hearts, our sincere pleas...we lift You on High, Adonai! We stand in awe of You, Your goodness that extends over time and has no boundary. We bask in the glow of Your radiance that pours forth from each creation...each whisper of beauty around us.

Protect us, my Lord, from hardening of heart and lost hope when the darkness of evil pants in the shadows. May we always know Your deliverance is at hand with a proclamation of Jesus!

The principalities and demons of Hates cower and fade at the sound of His Name. Hallelujah! Thank You for this life, for our families, for our experiences, for our provision, for our ability to worship, to read, to speak, to walk, to pray and for giving us the freedom to stand in Your Truth as we shout to the mountains "MOVE!" through the Spirit and the eternal existence of our Lord and Savior Christ Jesus, we make these pleas and lift Your glory to the Heavens.

Amen!

King David's Prayer

"Blessed be thou, Lord God of Israel our father, for ever and ever. Thine, O Lord is the greatness, and the power, and the glory, and the victory, and the majesty: for all that is in the heaven and in the earth is thine; thine is the kingdom, O Lord, and thou art exalted as head above all. Both riches and honour come of thee, and thou reignest over all; and in thine hand is power and might; and in thine hand it is to make great, and to give strength unto all. Now therefore, our God, we thank thee, and praise thy glorious name."

~ 1 Chronicles 29:10-13

IN PURSUIT OF BECOMING

a Serving Woman

INTRODUCTION
Why Serve?

The words in red show us what He designed us to be, how to act towards one another and provided us with such valuable insight into the Heart of Christ. As faithful servants of a most high God, we still all fall short at times and pigeon hole ourselves to 'serving' in such traditional and sometimes, limited ways.

Join me as we explore the servant heart of a Christ follower, some experiences I have had and what God has revealed to me in one of the most important area of our faith...serving!

> *"You, my brothers and sisters, were called to be free.*
> *But do not use your freedom to indulge the flesh; rather, serve one another humbly in love."*
>
> **~ Galatians 5:13**

HER SON

*O*VER HIS SHOULDER, HE saw her standing at the edge of the street as tears stained her cheeks; her eyes were full of fear as she met His glance. She sobbed silently to herself, "Oh, how could they do this!" Then she remembered what was said to her in the stillness of a night long ago.

Cries fueled by hate, a tirade of insults, a frenzy fueled by such blatant ignorance. The dust rose in the streets as they shouted louder and louder. Sand stung His eyes.

The muscles in His legs were weak…the pain in His back was unbearable…however, He walked on. His flesh was burning from the beatings and the heat of the sun pierced through His robe. So much shouting, yet only His own heartbeat was heard. The time, the distance, was ending. Looking up, He saw them staring. Solemn and cold. The shadows were familiar.

Exhausted, he dropped to His knees. They pushed Him onto the cross He carried. His back pressed against the hardness of the wood… His hands were pulled tightly away from Him. His feet, almost flattened, were being bent downward, yet He offered no resistance. No hesitation. Nothing but devotion to the Cause. Devotion to the end…to us.

Shards of metal shot through sinews of flesh like a hot iron racing pain up through His arms, up His legs, across His back. An awareness of what was happening overcame Him. Time stood still.

Gall drink...a whisper...His mother's eyes once again. Only moments stood in between His death and eternal life for all of mankind. They shouted, "Save yourself!" They mocked! But all He listened for was the voice of His Father. Crying out, He drew His last breath. It was finished.

The silence was then broken! They looked in horror and disbelief as the ground shook, the sky darkened, as the air thickened and panic rose throughout the land! People, for a fleeting minute after hours of chaos, fell speechless! Looking up...they wondered.

Was it true? Was it really true?!

Gently, she held Him in her arms and softly brushed His hair off of His eyes. Amid the blood, dirt, and sweat, His face shone with an innocence of a child sleeping in his mother's lap. How precious was her love for Him...how profound His love for us.

In that tiny tomb, He lay. In that darkness, He was covered with oils and perfume...the beautiful aroma filled the cavern. Within moments, the glimpse of His face would be forever etched in her memory. One last look. One last touch. One last kiss.

Then, in the cool of a morning three days later, He arose.

Her Son arose.

A Glimpse...

When my father became ill, I learned what selfless serving looked like. I watched how he was constantly prayed over, bed linens cleaned, every need met, and his wife made more personal sacrifices than we could count. I saw sleepless days pass, meals go to waste, and housework go undone. I tried to step in as much as possible and help, but somehow it all was miraculously handled. Right up to the time of his passing, I saw what serving your family looked like, but I was not as engaged as I wanted to be simply out of circumstance.

The grieving process was even more painful, as I truly went through it alone in my head. The years of memories and new seasons collided often, making it all seem so surreal.

That all changed when my mother became ill five years later.

What occurred to me, while I was helping my mother to her chair to have coffee, was the number of times during my life she served me. Understandably, she was my mother and it was her role to care for me, provide for me, not allow me harm, and ensure that my physical needs were being met.

That's not what I am referring to. She *served me*. She would do more than tend to me if I was sick, as she anticipated my needs, seeing clearly what was lacking and quickly closing the gap. She knew best how to serve others and give herself away completely.

After all, she dedicated her life to serving others. She was a nursing assistant for over thirty-eight years and possessed a gift of mercy for others like no one I have ever met. I watched how my brother toiled over her medication changes, dietary needs, and tried to encourage her to not just give up. The week prior to her passing, the level of service was unlike anything that I have ever taken part in. From complete care to ensuring the world around her continued to move, it was daunting.

My brother and I experienced the sleepless nights reminiscing of times past, laughing and then crying at the realization that Mom was part of those memories.

We painfully faced the reality of our mortality. I saw the stages of life, of death, and of grief unfold before my eyes. I could not fully grieve until over a year later because of some very painful circumstances surrounding the mess that was left behind, but I know God pushed me during this most tender season to show me what servitude looks like. Real servitude. Sacrifice amid isolation and constantly feeling overlooked.

These two very profound experiences educated me on serving my family. The untold moments of intense emotional darkness met with an unyielding grace that can only come from Him. Witnessing His glory in the throes of loss.

Salvation draws near for some during the times of seeking answers. His sovereignty becomes increasingly apparent. His mercy and grace then eclipse the pain. At that moment, you see Him.

Ever so clearly.

SERVING HIM THROUGH OUR FAMILY

*T*YPICALLY, WHEN ONE THINKS of serving, they may think of restaurant help, hotel housekeeping, or someone having live-in housemaids or an au pair for their children. Serving, as understood by worldly definition, consists of actions (services or duties) that are usually *in response to an expressed need*. Included in this same definition are phrases such as carry out wishes of another, contribute to, be obedient to, and minister to. Expansive, yet simple.

Variations of the verb serve (through words like work, subject, and worship) occur 284 times in 25 of the 39 different books of the Old Testament alone! How appropriate is it, the, to see how the greatest Servant of all manifested in flesh in the New Testament? Was the idea of serving reiterated repeatedly among scripture to help us prepare our hearts to receive from the One who laid His very life on a cross for us?

Do we serve the One who first loved us by loving our neighbor as ourselves, ensuring that we are last, and continue to be as diligent as the virtuous woman extensively described earlier?

If the answer is yes, then please sit down for this next statement. This includes your family.

> *"But if anyone does not provide for his relatives,*
> *and especially for members of his household,*
> *he has denied the faith and is worse than an*
> *unbeliever."*
>
> **~ 1 Timothy 5:8**

Through a variety of experiences, I have served. In the church, within my family, at work, and total strangers on the street. It was not until I noticed the *value* of serving did it occur to me that as we follow Christ, we are not only to always serve, but we must also be continuously *looking for* opportunities to serve. We must remain active in our faith; encouraging, uplifting, and imparting the wisdom manifested through our own trials onto others.

If we stay conscience in leveraging our experiences through serving, we will see more opportunities to do this. We will also see a higher level of faith develop.

After all, how can serving *not* growth our faith? We are surrounding ourselves in a position of serving the needs of our fellow man while conveying the very heart of Jesus. In doing that, we operate in the Spirit and like His word, the efforts do not return void. The fact remains; however, that the rewards may not be seen in this lifetime. Not that we serve for the benefit to self but understanding God's blessings will flow back to us for our heartfelt efforts. An eternal reward awaits us and, for that alone, we can remain steadfast in our service.

> *"What good is it, my brothers, if someone says*
> *he has faith but does not have works? Can that*
> *faith save him? If a brother or sister is poorly*
> *clothed and lacking in daily food, and one of*
> *you says to them, 'Go in peace, be warmed and*

> *filled,' without giving them the things needed for the body, what good is that? So also, faith by itself, if it does not have works, is dead."*
>
> ~ **James 2: 14-17**

In my experience, times serving my family has proven to be the most tested periods for my faith.

I recall serving my father before he passed and having the dynamics of his wife and her family to contend with. These strangers were staples of my father's life when we were estranged and knew him well. I suffered watching their faces look upon my father with such grief, yet I was dying inside feeling left out of a decade of life experiences! Serving in this vacuum was unique and, frankly, extremely lonely.

Seeing my father, a formerly active and virile man his whole life, reduced to such weakness in his body was not only heart wrenching, but also an experience that I did not share with my siblings or even my adult son at the time. His mind was intact and so was his sense of humor, but I could see the brokenness in his eyes. The wonder and shock of the life that he led so proudly coming to a close. A very painful close. And fast.

I helped as I could. I remember trying to make him lunch and suddenly feeling inept to even scramble an egg for him! I pressed on to make him coffee, then offered him ice cream. With such grace in his smile, he accepted. He knew that this menu was not a menu for the ill, but he saw my heart and *willingness to help*. My dad knew I loved him, and his eyes pierced my very soul each time he would look at me. His gratitude was genuine. His need was great and, although he took me up on my offer to assist him, deep down I could tell it was breaking him to be seen in this way.

Think about the last time you asked for real help. Think about the humility in your heart at that moment. The fear, maybe, of being told no. Unless you really know the person that you asked for help or if they really know you, chances are, it was hard to ask. Chances are, there was a bit of shame or pride that rose up before you asked. There is not supposed to be that kind of hindrance with family, right? Well, sometimes there is.

Sometimes, the offer to assist comes way after the need is even mentioned. The offer to assist is met with staunch pride, stubbornness and embarrassment. Family can display these traits without being in need; however, what if they magnified even more during a time of distress? How would you feel about serving then?

> *"Bear one another's burdens,*
> *and so fulfill the law of Christ."*
>
> ~ **Galatians 6:2**

Yes, the fulfillment of Him.

It can be hard. It can be emotionally draining. It can expose you to abuse, belittlement, isolation, and conjure up all kinds of memories of that family member with whom you still need to reconcile.

Serve anyway.

Whether it is staying in some hotel hours from home for five days and leaving work unattended like I did when my son was in an accident or maybe it is staying in a hotel for only one night, rushing to the side of your injured Mother only be told coldly to leave. The ability to serve and the willingness to do so was in both scenarios. One was met with gratitude, love, and a rekindled bonding, and the other was met with hostile pride and self-pity. Both were serving opportunities, and both were experiences that drew me even closer to Christ!

In one case, I was brought to a realization of God's sovereignty while laying on my face in the church sanctuary and in the other case, experiencing God's protection by hearing Him say, "Go home," while holding the hotel Bible in my hands! (Sadly, the next morning my Mother told me the same thing.)

Years later, I would be by my Mother's side as she drew her last breath and then continue to serve the family tirelessly until eventually God stopped me. Unfortunately, the level of servitude, mercy, and grace hit its pivotal end.

But God.

Earlier this year, my son and his beautiful fiancé gave birth to my first grandchild. In this most joyous event, there was an opportunity to serve their new family during a time of their greatest need. I not only relished the idea of helping them in any capacity that I could, I met God in those moments filled with stillness and prayer for our new baby. I tended to my needs as they arose and, unlike times in the past, I knew of the crucial need for self-care not so that I would be fully functional, but that I would be FULLY AVAILABLE!

> *"Beloved, I pray that all may go well with you and that you may be in good health, as it goes well with your soul."*
> **~ 3 John 1:2**

Not only did I need to have my health intact while I served my son's family, I also needed to take the time to pray, be in His word, and prepare at any time to give hope or encouragement during the trying time we experienced. My soul needed to be fed, nurtured, and in a position of receiving from Christ so I could best *serve*.

Keeping a priority to the most important ministry of your life, your family, will honor God greatly. Ministry begins at home and throughout

Scripture, the very Word of God was handed down through generations inside of families! It was up to the bloodline to keep going in the Old Testament and along with those historic lineages was the concept of serving within the family.

Although there are a multitude of examples we can pull from, one that stands out is Ruth *choosing to stay with and serve* Naomi. Naomi was clear that she was aged and could not bear anymore sons for Ruth (even *if* Ruth could wait for them) and that her obligation to the family line was over. Ruth pleaded. Ruth insisted. Ruth followed.

Ruth served not only Naomi, but also her future husband, Boaz. Her grief was sizeable at the beginning of the story, but her sorrow led to service which led to restoration. A lineage that would eventually birth Christ, the greatest of all servants!

Our service can lend an influence in our own family's lineage. One will not know until many years later, if at all. Either way, we honor God by serving our family and setting the winds in motions to blow blessings over the lives of those we are not only called to love, but also have been given the privilege to.

Let's Pray

Most anointed One! To You, Oh God, we come and thank You for your greatest service to us- Your Son's life for ours! Jesus, through Your sacrifice and ultimate service to mankind, You have given us eternal life.

You call us friend; however, we are also Your brethren, co-heirs of a Kingdom that we do not deserve. You have shown us how to serve. You knelt before Your disciples that fateful night and washed their very feet! How humble and yet how strong You served the ones that walked with You. They ate with You. They ventured with You. Yet, one sinned against You greatly, but even for him, You died.

My God, we come before You and ask You, to help us serve with grace, humility, love and most of all, with the light of Jesus in all we do! Jesus served and died without expectation. Help us serve without expectations as well, Lord knowing that You see it all. Every action, every thought, every silent prayer, every unfilled need, every sacrifice we make...You see it!

Our families are grafted into our hearts and even times of most difficulty, their pain is our pain. We suffer with them, Lord. Even in those darkest hours, You see the pride or the resistance we face. In those times, soften their hearts, Lord. May they receive the same agape love You wish to give them through us.

For the family that we serve daily, give them eyes to see the loving sacrifice and honor You for it. May we serve always unto You, Oh Lord and we pray that You reward us according to Your abundant riches, both here on Earth and in Heaven when we receive our jewels. As we stand in the gap for our beloved ones, gird us up with strength to remain steadfast in prayer for their needs or for their protection from the enemy during their times of weakness.

May Your power manifest greatly in these times and we give You all the honor and glory for it!

Amen.

A Glimpse...

Over the course of many years, I have seen ministries come and go. I have seen church attendance in both small and large churches fluctuate dramatically outside of the predictable Easter, Christmas, and summer seasons. I have seen program-driven methods of enticing newcomers have *some* success, but eventually either fade out or lose church funding along the way. I have seen the fallout of all these things and watched while the seeker, the seasoned, and the saddened wander away from the church altogether because of it.

I've been introduced to the term 'voluntold,' meaning the hybrid of asking for someone's assistance and the declaration that there *really isn't anyone else to ask,* so YOU are it! When a church resorts to this tactic, it doesn't always pertain to a lack of capable and willing volunteers, but instead reflects that leadership recognizes a person's gifting in an area of need and simply matches the crucial with the resource! If that isn't the case, then we are left with the broken reality that there *does exist* a gap of help from the body to fulfill even basic volunteer roles.

When this happens, the church as a whole hurts. The regular body suffers from not being properly (or even ambivalently) served by those whom have already surpassed their given level of grace and are, out of obligation, burned out! The ones seeking a church home or even an encounter with the Living God during a season of their lives are impacted by the lack. They are not met with the anticipation or excitement that God welcomes them in the doors or even worse, have an incredible experience that becomes altered by an entitled group of church regulars.

This section of my book has taken me the longest to write as God was pulling me through some experiences that would show me about serving in the Church. I have, in the last six months, been through some rigorous physical tasks for God's people and have seen the both the humility in receiving and have witnessed the unfortunate entitlement that pride offers even to the saved.

This dichotomy brings with it a fresh revelation of the human spirit and exposes a new stretch of faith within me that I did not know I possessed. It has been only through God's grace and redemptive power can I say that I did not walk away from the call over my life during this season as some of the shocking realities of serving God's people almost did me in!

Although I saw the drudgery, the angst, the ungrateful, the untruthful, and sometimes the brokenness that exists on not only on the side of those being served, but on the side of those serving, I still praise God that I GET to serve!

SERVING HIM THROUGH OUR CHURCH

My spiritual father requisitioned me to conduct a training on serving and through the pages of notes he furnished me, I found layers of cerebral data that could help a lay person understand the concept of serving, but soon realized the deeper connection to serving would only come through a revelation of heart and THAT is not something that can be taught! It can only be CAUGHT!

In honoring God, our lead pastor and the very house of God to which I have been assigned in this season, I welcome this revelation to not only allow me to serve more effectively but also to pass on to my peers these truths.

For instance, serving in a local ministry capacity several times in my Christian life I have seen others serve out of obligation. They attempt to look good in front of the church leaders and leverage the opportunity to showcase *themselves* during service to others. I have been on the receiving end of probing questions asking where I am serving, if I can do more because they are short in other areas, all the while reminding me that my overextension of self was in line of what the leaders expected. In other words, increased works for the sake of saving face in the church!

Where as soon as your service becomes lessened, so did acknowledgement of who you were. Pulling back from serving in some capacities due to life demands and unequal yoking of gifts was met with distancing and ostracizing from church members. As a result, I've seen people serve unhappily in this capacity.

They are doing a favor for the leaders, not serving for the right reasons, and just to fulfill some social requirement. What the byproduct of that type of service can bring is a self-righteous and entitled attitude. It empowers pride and condemnation among the group of those serving towards those unable to serve or towards those who can only serve in a smaller capacity. I've seen the hurt it produces among those who are called to serve when they are shunned or pushed aside for someone else to gain recognition.

This type of service exists, Sisters, and I am here to tell you from a position of authority in Christ that it isn't holy and it isn't honoring God! In these cases, a level of deliverance and breaking free from strongholds may be required to freely love oneself, love others, and trust in the discerning of the Spirit to guide both leadership and those called to serve.

Unfortunately, I have seen those who were being served take on an entitled attitude and even be openly ungrateful or greedy! I have seen the church or ministry become the victim of such callousness and selfishness, but rest on the fact that our God sees it all and will reward the church for its faithfulness.

I have witnessed theft, blasphemy, cruelty, and egoism revolt against me while I am literally serving someone to the best of my ability. Speechless, I stood there. Hurt, confused, and bordering angry, I said nothing. I just kept serving. The suppressed pain, disappointment, and disenchantment almost broke me. I knew that my hardest work for the Kingdom would bless someone and that God would vindicate me! I also knew that this exposure to being hurt was a hearty reminder that I must be continually dying to myself and my flesh.

Without actively participating in this ongoing consecration, I would be left feeling a way that did not reflect the heart of the Father or His intentions for the service of the Church. I would be left with a victim mentality and open fodder for the evil one!

> "But he gives more grace. Therefore, it says,
> 'God opposes the proud, but gives grace to the humble.'"
>
> ~ **James 4:6**

See, spiritual warfare threatens the work of God and no place is exempt! As God is watching over and bringing recompense to the situation, Satan still tries to make his presence known. It is then, with a sound mind and the indwelling power of Christ, we must remain diligent in prayer as we serve. The evil one does not take a day off at any time and will attempt to *steal* joy brought about from serving, *kill* momentum in service, and *destroy* the goals the church sets out to accomplish!

When there is a true yielding to the Spirit of God, His glory manifests in a multitude of ways, my friend. One's faith grows because of serving as they may encounter the very face of God when a brother's needs are met at their hands. They may be called to further influence them by offering specific prayer and a call to receive Christ! I've served on homeless missions where those who came for a hot meal left with so much more!

They left with the knowing of Christ, the acceptance of His sacrifice, and belief that they, too, will have eternal life! I've seen faces change. Tears well up and beautifully flow down the cheeks of someone who has been living on the streets for months. All because a heartfelt child of God extended themselves to the body of Christ by serving and often by serving in a capacity that no one else wanted to.

> *"Take delight in the LORD,*
> *and he will give you the desires of your heart."*
> **~ Psalm 37:4**

His word reminds us to delight ourselves in Him and He gives us the desires of our hearts. Often do we realize how much God sees within us and then, when the time comes for selfless service, we experience His hand over our deepest concerns? He fulfills our dreams! All He asks is for obedience. Truthful, willful obedience.

Let's Pray

Father, boldly we approach the Throne of grace asking You to reveal to us our very heart for Your people! In serving, we sometimes fall short to see the bigger picture that it is for the sake of Your children's souls. Help us recall that we are called to a Purpose. Your purpose for not only our lives but for the lives of those in which we serve! Help us, O' Lord, to remember such things begin and end in Heaven, are governed by Your grace, mercy, endurance, and Spirit and not by our own flesh or might.

Lord, You show us time and time again where we can step outside of ourselves and lend a hand to a fellow brother and the fulfilment is not just immediate, but Lord, we trust that you will show its ripple effect to the ends of the earth!

We pray that somehow, we are steadied to see the manifestation of Your Spirit in our hands and in our hearts. Tears of joy stream down our face in humility to the Call! Stop us when we attempt to see our service as just another way of advertising our works, our goodness, and our flesh; instead, help us not call attention to the right hand's workings and allow Your Spirit to flow through blessings according to Your great plan. We also endure, O' Lord. We become broken at times and we suffer for Your sake, but we count it all joy! We relish the fragrance of You in our lives, Jesus.

Great Abba, may all Your children see to it that they serve and love one another as You commanded so long ago. We pray against the wiles, assignments, and destruction of the enemy to plot pride, false humility, and self-gain in serving. We banish his attempts to thwart Your children to serve from the depths of their souls and not from a superficial surface. Legalism, religion, and tradition be broken NOW in the name of Christ Jesus as we seek to place You, Your children, and Your will ahead of anything we claim to follow.

Guide us. Move us. Empower us with the same Spirit that raised Your Son from the grave! May we act justly, love mercifully, and walk humbly with You, O' God, all the days of our lives! To the Glory of our Father in Heaven we pray.

Amen!

A Glimpse...

Throughout career changes, God led me to both challenging times and times filled with purposeful revelation. Both ends of this spectrum have offered me profound lessons in humanity and seeing sometimes the complexity of God. I witnessed His network of moves within my life, and watched His delicate choreography come alive as He led me through trials and successes alike! This dichotomy has, at times, blown me away with favor and humbled me during correction.

I've held positions where leading others was easy and yielded both financial and career-enhancing benefits. I have been able to buy homes, multiple cars, and had the ability to buy the best of everything my heart desired. I have also transitioned away from those same positions and found myself struggling to make ends meet and left to sell several garages full of belongings to pay the bills. Where I laid my affections, my time, and my attention, is where I typically felt I had the most security.

It was not until the time that I began to lose it all that I realized that my only true Security was there the whole time; regrettably unacknowledged. Not until I was hands to Heaven, knees to the floor in repentance did I see the mercy and grace of a loving Father that I took for granted.

Aside from the material aspects of wealth and the subsequent loss of it, I also bore witness to my inner most thoughts and the analysis of my actions. Why was I so much more efficient at my jobs than I was at being an efficient housewife, and why did I take such great pride in *my* work and not in *other's* work? Where did the entire thought process come from and how did it fit into God's plan for my life? Did I give God the glory He deserved while leading people, coaching for improvement, and climbing the corporate ladder? Was I acknowledging His workings in my life, or was I simply leaning onto my own understanding?

Was I even serving Him as I was busy from my day to day? If so, HOW was I doing that?

When confronted with the sobering realization that even among the duties outlined in my job description, I also had the ability to SERVE Him in a whole different way. That one thought changed the trajectory of my secular career forever.

It changed the level of influence, level of engagement, and awakened in me biblical principles that were to not only be applied to my daily choices but also to the interactions with those people I was called to serve in my workplace.

SERVING HIM THROUGH OUR WORK

"Whatever you do, work at it with all your heart, as working for the Lord, not for human masters..."

~ **Colossians 3:23**

$\mathcal{S}$ERVING THE LORD IN all we do seems to be a straightforward command of the gospels. However, speaking only from my own vantage point, I can tell you that I struggled with this for years when it came to my vocation as it took me years to see my labor as a form of worship and service unto God.

I have worked for a version of Pharaoh in Exodus 5, having the dwindling resources disregarded while we still needed to fulfil an ever-increasing demand of *something*! I listened to the hypocrisy of the greater good depicting the overarching goals set forth by the upper echelon of organizations that never sought to understand the daily challenges of making those visions manifest in the first place. Embittered, deflated, and void of any self- esteem, I labored on half-heartedly.

Those who expected something in return for their help were in constant touch to remind me of my pay back and lorded over me accordingly. I was constantly brought into circumstances to help repair debacles caused by someone else, yet I rarely received recognition for my work or saw any level of accountability brought forth to the guilty party. Instead, I created a reputation of one who will step in and fix things, which may have brought me a financial increase, but what was exchanged for it I came to only understand later.

I recall having the concept of serving in my workplace introduced to me by a spiritual mentor as "Servant Leadership." This concept of leadership is rarely seen in modern businesses and not as present in large, corporate environments. It is not taught. It *is*; however, caught. Working for someone who emulated this concept changed my mindset considerably about what true leadership looked like. This individual focused on ensuring that the obstacles that interfered with the ability of his workforce to complete their tasks were effectively removed.

He worked to tirelessly install trust by being consistent and fair in all matters. He ruled by his heart but played by the rules. He ushered in a way of placing others first and working hard to disband selfishness and immaturity within the leadership staff.

He strived to be like Jesus Christ, who was the perfect example of this type of leadership. Jesus displayed acts of service without any hesitation; healing the sick, giving the blind the ability to see, imparting wholeness to the lame and dispatching deliverance to those tormented by evil. He washed the feet of the disciples, He spoke directly to the unnamed woman in Luke 7, and created leaders out of ordinary men. He placed the carnal needs of His own behind Him through great temptation in the desert with His adversary and embodied long suffering in a variety of ways. He humbly set Himself last.

*"So the last shall be first, and the first last:
for many be called, but few chosen."*
~ **Matthew 20:16**

Because of what He has done, He did not boast. He did not feel entitled for recognition over dying for our sins because it was ***in service*** to our Heavenly Father that He did so! Through hardship, uncertainty, having been accused of blasphemy, being betrayed, carrying a cross while being physically afflicted, bearing the effects of false-witness against Him, and enduring mockery and arrows of the enemy at every turn, Jesus was ***in service!***

I do not know about you, Sister, but those ideas resonated deeply within me. I came to see that in leadership, I will face the same, if not worse, and through my working relationship with imperfect people, just like myself, I would endure many of the same things. And I did.

I had to begin to see my work as an assignment from God and, since He is sovereign, I came to understand that He allowed me to be present in my workplace for a greater good than I may have ever seen. My purpose and call to my workplace was for the sake of doing *His work*. Yes, there were charts, bar graphs, meetings, dissertations, analysis, assessments, reports, teambuilding, and physical labor beyond what I was able to do effectively, plots against my good works, defaming my intentions, accusations of evil doing, and so much more. But, again, all parts of my assignment were to be completed. Through God I was able to endure all these things as is was He who gave me strength.

In my flesh, I wrestled with the balance between staying focused on the task at hand and trying not to let the subtle intimidation of others derail me from a greater purpose. I stood down from enticements of arguing, belittlement and a pulling by evil spirits to lose my footing of integrity. Edified on one hand for my way with words to diffuse situations and then strategized against for it. While I, at times, focused my eyes on the enemy lines, little did I realize the multitude of faithful witnesses that were watching (Much to my surprise the loyalty that was being born out of my testimony and constant extension of grace!). Those who lacked integrity in what they did were no longer a focus of my fight. The wrestling of principalities and evil spirits were my sole targets and God would take care of the rest.

And He did.

> *"Repay no one evil for evil but give thought to do what is honorable in the sight of all. If possible, so far as it depends on you, live peaceably with all. Beloved, never avenge yourselves, but leave it to the wrath of God, for it is written, 'Vengeance is mine, I will repay, says the Lord.' To the contrary, 'if your enemy is hungry, feed him; if he is thirsty, give him something to drink; for by so doing you will heap burning coals on his head. Do not be overcome by evil but overcome evil with good.'"*
>
> ~ **Romans 12:17-21**

I began to see that fruit needed to be harvested in the fields that were presented to me. For every conversation had over the watercooler, in my office during a lunch break or after work when someone was hurting, I took the chance to pour into a soul. With an assignment attached to each person, God reflected in me what I had grown to learn about truly serving at work; people *don't stop* being people when they walk into the building in the morning. Their lives play out before them in-between calls, emails, and meetings. Prayer vigils in bathroom stalls for people battling divorce, addiction, death, and lost hopes. Although there were times throughout my career that I saw the makings of spiritual warfare at hand, I remained vigilant in prayer for authority in my workplace. Spirits of pride, jealousy, and even a strong anti-Christ spirit was often present. Communications were muffled, intentions were questions, and characters were basically assassinated.

Disheartened, but true to a cause to reflect the light and hope for Christ in all I did, I pressed on. I continued to pray that He give me more chances to navigate in His will even when it was uncomfortable.

> *"For everyone born of God overcomes the world. This is the victory that has overcome the world, even our faith."*
> ~ **1 John 5:4**

Ultimately, I knew that no matter what, God helped me hold my peace when I was discouraged and helped me remain in grace when my flesh was weak from unfair treatment. I knew that what God was using to stretch or challenge me, and I would grow exponentially from it. From what I thought was taken from me in ways of dignity, honor, or respect, God multiplied it back to me when He blessed me with a change of direction.

> *"Very truly I tell you, whoever believes in me will do the works I have been doing, and they will do even greater things than these..."*
> ~ **John 14:12**

Walking in true purpose, I knew that although I did what I could to set Godly examples in my work, striving for excellence in all I accomplished, not everyone would be impressed or even impacted. I had to work unto the Lord knowing that I was given the same power that Jesus had from the sting of death and I could hold my head up high.

I prayed for my leaders as God placed them in those roles to begin with, and it was my honor to petition the Lord to guide them, quicken their hearts to soften towards their people, and make the best decisions they knew to make. It may not have made a large difference to them personally, but that was not what was important. It was following the prompting of the Spirit to intercede, lift, and edify those in authority even when I didn't want to. It was my call, my duty, my command.

I understand from many who have taken positions of leadership that often they are faced with immeasurable stress, personal sacrifices that can only be experienced to be understood, and wrestle with the human conditions of the heart of the people they are called to lead. I have been there and walked in those shoes for many years. Just because someone is elevated in a business does not constitute the fact that they have arrived at point, but that they are just accepting the call to shepherd people.

Not everyone knows what that truly looks like and each corporation could interpret how they are different from the rest. Ultimately, if a leader governs their actions by the only Book that grounds itself in total morality, authority, and truth, their decisions will be based on Godly principles and the people will flourish. If not, then it will always be a struggle.

Even as those who may fall under the authority of others, we can secure our footing in the Lord by remaining steadfast in prayer, abiding to the decrees, rules and bylaws set before us, and trusting the Lord. He will arrange favor, clarity, and blessings for our obedience if we are unshakeable in our faith. He may also call you to a new season or assignment and once you are confirmed before the Lord on such bold moves, you must act swiftly.

Personally, I left corporate America last year when the Lord showed me that my vocation in full-time ministry would take me deeper in communion with Him and I would embark on a journey where my trust in Him would be truly tested. Although I assisted another ministry for a time being after I left, God used that experience to just remind me that I had an undergirding endurance that was powerful! He broke within me places where I came to understand what true service looked like and where a religious mindset can derail God's plan for a ministry. Regardless, I learned, spoke my truth, and extinguished the arrows of the enemy as I entered a new season of renewal.

> *"And we know that God causes everything to work together for the good of those who love God and are called according to his purpose for them."*
> **~ Romans 8:28**

Sister, allow me to leave you with this thought; when your God-given abilities intersect with your Spirit-given gifts, your possibilities are endless. Your potential to rise closer to the calling that God has on your life becomes even greater and no demon in Hell can stop you! You must believe you can walk fully in the purpose of your life no matter who you work for or where you work. You employ all the excellence that is within you, you eagerly serve those that Lead you and obediently, you trust God to help you soar to the heights that He wants to take you. He furnishes you with peace, grace, and mercy every day. He equips you with a sound mind and a spirit of boldness, not timidity.

Own and multiply these truths by simple *influence*. Godly influence that no policy, procedure, or work rule can ever take from you. Godly influence that reflects the heart of our Lord and Savior, Christ Jesus, and demonstrates one of the greatest loves of all; Service to one another.

Let's Pray

El Shaddai, I thank You for this revelation of Spirit that I can share with my readers today. I pray Lord that although we struggle with what we feel is injustice sometimes in our employment, is just You speaking to us through lessons, correction, discipline, or just loving us through the very acts of submission. After all, Your Son, Christ Jesus, was the greatest Servant of all, and even through Pharisee mindsets, insults, mockery, betrayal, and ostracizing, He performed the greatest act of service to us all!

He died so we can live more abundantly and take part of all the blessings that Heaven has to offer. I know God that there are those that have been struggling to find their purpose, their life call and their place in a vocation and I ask You now to help them realign themselves with You.

Quicken their hearts to live more intentionally for You. I pray that they enter Your gates with praise more often and find You waiting still for them in the very hour of their need! I pray that You have mercy on their authority figures that may have taken them for granted and know not their hearts. I know that You will stand in the gap for them and provide every need for them according to Your glorious riches in Christ.

You are Jehovah Jireh! I trust You and I pray that because of my testimony and experiences, that others will be more willing to trust You too with their every need, coming to understand that You are the one true Source for everything!

I lift every leader that reads this today and hope they see that they need to work by the principles of Your Word for the better of the people they have been assigned to. I pray that they rest in Your planned promises to prosper them and give them a future! Submission to Your will leads to obedience and a heartfelt repentance to restore what has been lost.

You are a faithful God and we adore You! To the power and glory forever we pray through the Spirit in the name of Christ Jesus.

Amen.

#FAITHWALKER

*G*REETINGS IN THE NAME of our Lord Jesus Christ, our true Savior! I just wanted to offer a small word of advice… "Walk in your faith." Yes, that's it. Short and simple.

Admit it, we all have that faith that keeps us in our seats every Sunday, on our knees at the altar and can speak to it, sing about it, and emblazon it across a cute T-shirt, but how many of us can say that aside from the few times that you have boldly walked in faith, and that it is a true habit?

Okay, assuming at least one of you pointed shyly to yourself, I will continue.

For months now, the Lord has been priming me for something aside from my call as a pastor, but to an end that I am slowly being enlightened on. As the revelation became increasingly clear, I have been torn to move forward to full-time ministry. See, I loved my secular job as an analyst and I was always learning something new and developing my skill sets. What became difficult was feeling the truest ALIVE in an environment that simply did not produce LIFE. Several times, the Lord showed me what operating in my fullest capacity would be like having the opportunity to run at full speed with reckless abandon on a never-ending shoreline.

The freedom, the wind against my back, and the ability to navigate solely on where He takes me! But how can I aid the homeless, pour hope into the widow, pray for those in need, conduct studies, give sermons, or help a single mom with her resume when I am working forty hours a week? When was I to LEAP into the vocation of pastor? I certainly know that I could not do it without the assurance and leading of God Himself.

He then began clearly showing me sign after sign. He gave me not a spirit of apathy, but one of conviction that I truly was needed elsewhere, and there was a host of Kingdom work to be done whilst I worked away seemingly in vain. Then, suddenly, a gaping hole in peace surfaced and without question, I stood, raised my hand and had an **Isaiah 6** moment: "Send me, Lord…I will go!" As soon as the first item was shoveled into a box, peace overcame me. A resounding peace that I have not felt outside of my own ordination into the pastorate this year. Not an uneasiness. Not a panic (although I passed by a sign that literally read "Has the panic set in yet?"). Nothing but a peace and a bullet in my britches to go…I mean Go; no, I mean GO, RIGHT NOW! And so, I did.

I drove straight to my husband's job. Seeing his face was enough for me. The true abandon; the faithful fall into the arms of Jesus; the complete and utter surrender – LITERALLY all of what He has entrusted to us. In my husband's smile was the confirmation. Our marriage realigned! My joy will be restored! My health will be restored! My motherhood will be revived! My friendships will be highlighted! My service to the body will come alive…alive as God intended.

Sharing my news with a chosen few, being transparent and quick to give God His due glory, one sister in the faith shot back a few loving words of encouragement, along with the phrase, #FaithWalker. Wow. Of all things to be called, THIS is the most powerful. The one that resonates to my very marrow. So as I embark in this next for my life, my marriage, my ministry, and following the path that God leads me down, I step in faith. Bold, ridiculous, mind-blowing, soul-lifting, focus-driven, spirit-filled faith!

A Glimpse...

Part of my story is the season in which my son, Brandon served in the Iraq war in 2009. Having given my life back to Christ was a huge part of that season and because I was faced with the possibility of danger for my only child, I clung to the only thing I knew was left-faith. Praise God that I did as my life has never been the same since! I wrote earlier about how I became connected to a Life Group, a Bible-based church and some very faithful mentors. During that same time, I was learning how to trust God for the safe return of my son. Every prayer request was about him.

Every time that I saw anything on the news related to the war, my heart skipped a beat. My mother at the time would always remind me that she was praying and that she felt that God would not only return Brandon back to me, but that he would also someday become a great man for the Kingdom. I recall that same promise being poured into my spirit one day during worship service and the overwhelming peace I felt when it pierced my soul.

What a glorious feeling even now that I write this as I see God's promises manifesting before me.

My Life Group decided to create a video for the troops for Veteran's Day. When the inspiration hit me, I wrote the following script in honor of those serving. It was also in honor of my son.

I realize that I may be one of the lucky ones that had a loved one return from war. I realize that the very fact that I can hold him in my arms is more than a blessing that I would ever dare to take for granted again. I realize that many of you may not have that luxury. My heart cries out for you. My heart knows the abundant love for a child and the zeal we have when we desire wholeness, health and prosperity for them. My heart is however, unfamiliar with that hope being deferred.

But, my soul is sure of this, my friend. If you lost a loved one during an act of service to our Country, know that our God is still a merciful God. He is a loving and adoring God that holds your tears in the palms of His hands and those same hands cradle your loved one now. See, they are His children before they are ours and He has a plan and purpose for all things.

Although a small and naively written script, my heart yearned for a connection with my son at the time and for that, I am unashamed. For without this gesture, someone in his platoon may not have received hope that day. That one soldier may have decided to follow this Christ we speak of. There may have been an intended audience of many, but if only one is reached, then I have lived out what Paul speaks of in 1 Corinthians 14, "Let Love be your greatest aim..."

Amen.

TO OUR SOLDIERS OF WAR

*D*URING WAR, WE AS a people, have at times not realized what privileges we have...what sacrifices our troops have made. When my son was at war, I wrote this in honor of him. For all of those who have served, are serving and are new to their assignment, this goes out to YOU! I know that Freedom isn't free and thank God for you!

Every day, most of us have the privilege of choice in what we do and where we go.

> *Your every action and move are dictated by*
> *offensive caution or military strategy.*

We have a freedom of prayer almost anywhere.
> *You are amid a Holy war every day.*

There are times when we complain how hot it is or how tired we are.
> *You carry gear equal to your weight in extreme*
> *conditions.*

We groan when we don't get a good night's rest and must go to work tired.
> *Most of you sleep in tents, if at all and deprive your body of needful rest.*

We complain over how little we are paid or how many obligations we have.
> *For a modest salary, you risk your life every day for responsibilities we cannot even fathom!*

We skip a meal and think we will starve of hunger.
> *Rations are your dinners and you dream of having a home-cooked meal!*

We may slack off at work for a few hours.
> *For you, that may mean death.*
> You are husbands, wives, brothers, sisters, fathers, mothers, sons, and daughters.
> You are honored.
> You are brave.
> You are highly favored.
> You are strong.
> You are loved.
> You are under His covering.
> You are mighty warriors.
> You are elite.
> You are admired.
> You are obedient.
> You are saints.
> You are the chosen few.

You are in the middle of God's will for not only your life, but for the lives of your fellow countrymen.

Today and every day, we honor you! Without your faithful service and selfless sacrifice, Veteran's Day as we know it would not exist. I have faith in a powerful God that will bring each of you home safely to your families.

Let's Pray

Heavenly Father, we pray a hedge of protection remain around these brave men and women and Your merciful hand lead their direction from the snares of the enemy. May Your wisdom strengthen and sharpen the minds of their leaders. May Your mercy heal their hearts, giving them comfort and rest in You. We pray Your power indwell their spirits as they seek You during these times of uncertainty.

You are a consistent and faithful God, yearning to hear us call Your name. You are beside their families, comforting them and giving them peace as they trust in Your amazing promise. We lift each of them up in prayer, calling each of them as children of a sovereign Lord who knows them each by name!

May all the powers of darkness that taunt the sanctification of Your faithful servants, flee in the name of Jesus Christ! We pray all these things in Your Son's precious name.

AMEN!

Be strong; know that God loves you and that you are appreciated! May you shine brightly into a world that WILL someday come to know peace!

DEAR DAUGHTER,

I AM AWARE OF THAT deep yearning for a fire to begin in your heart to stop you from being settled in what is around you, instead allowing you to learn more about yourself and those steps that I have asked you to take. This fire begins stoking a flame that touches the very heart of what you can see, touch, and hear. There is much that I want to show you, but will you go? Lift your hand and see My hand reaching for you. Can you smell the incense? The sweet aroma of My courtyard should set you at ease as you can finally feel the comfort you've longed for since you were small. Remember the heavens at night? Remember when you would gaze at the stars and the moon, wondering what else the night held? You looked up then, as you do now, and asked Me to speak to you. You wondered where life would lead you; if you would make it out alive.

Although the flames grow taller, you are not concerned with whether that they will burn you. That is good, my Daughter. You are learning to trust me with your passion. Allow me to manifest before you in My way to guide you to the next part of your journey.

This fire also burns a mote of protection around you. A hedge that is strictly there to keep the enemy out. It is there to further sanctify you, purify you, keep you holy, righteous, and separated from the folly that seems to be taking over the atmosphere around you. Can you feel the stillness? This shouldn't alarm you. This fire will pierce the grey and guide you, beloved.

Boldly, now you are ablaze. Every fiber of your being tingles. You become aware that you are not alone. The tips of the wings can be seen just outside of your peripheral. Daughter, did you notice? I've dispatched one to help you. To minister to you when you feel weak, and to war on your behalf when the enemy takes notice.

Love me with abandon, My child. Go do what I have called you to do. I will equip you, I will mount you upon the wings of an eagle, just like My word says. With Me, there is freedom. Trust Me that My love for you will never change. You will just begin to realize the depth, width and breadth of it, child.

Trust Me.
GOD

EPILOGUE

I pray that throughout this book, you have found a common thread sewn among its pages and within my story. I pray that with God's help, I have been able to bring light into places that perhaps darkness has laid stake to far too long. I pray that given my call to ministry and the impartation I've experienced; my life's mission statement became evident to you. Below is my personal mission statement, and this book is yet another extension of this commitment to Him and the work He has assigned me.

Whether it is a next book, a speaking engagement, or a prayer call that you participate in from my personal ministry, Daughters In Christ, Inc. or witness the Spirit of God using me in any way while in the mission field, it is my heart's desire that these statements are brought to life before you...

> *My mission is to consistently stay aware to the prompting of the Holy Spirit, obediently serving His people with an unconditional mercy and compassion. I will honestly communicate the word of God without bias or condemnation,*

but with a reverence to the inerrant truth of the Gospel and passionate conviction in relaying it.

I will strive to establish balance between intimate personal spiritual growth and careful encouragement for other women to nurture their spiritual growth and to stay true to the sacred family dynamic as ordained by God.

I will encourage women everywhere to build a home so anointed by the grace of God that they will become a formidable enemy of Satan, effectively tearing down strongholds and abolishing lies that have been so pervasive throughout family generations.

I will seek first to understand before being understood, permitting God's grace to flow through my words and actions. There will be a deep appreciation for God's favor and a reciprocal display of my gratitude towards His faithfulness by diligent stewardship and sharing of His provision when prompted by the Holy Spirit.

I commit to be of a sound and peaceful heart, establishing a ministry of love, acceptance, honesty, trust, humor, and an unbridled passion for the love of Christ in all I do! I will remind women that we are all God's children and, as in His image, we need to hold each other accountable in maintaining this despite hardships, trials and testing.

As a faithful Daughter of a Most High God, I commit to be a foundation support beam to God's growing family tree, committing to strength-training within His Word. As I share my faith with a sometimes dark and hopeless world, I will stay true to our God as a willing vessel and instrument of change, allowing Him to speak through me. His Great Commission is my call and I trust His equipping as I travel through this amazing life He has given me.

Lastly, I strongly and openly commit to bold evangelical ministry fueled by fervency and trust in God's lighting of my every step!

ABOUT THE AUTHOR

As CEO and founder of Daughters In Christ, Inc. – A Christian Ministry for Women, Pastor Sandra Astacio currently serves as a spiritual mentor for many women who seek a deeper relationship with God. Through speaking engagements, biblical studies, individual counsel and career preparation workshops, she has dedicated her life to INSPIRING, ENCOURAGING AND EMPOWERING women to reach for all that God has in store for them as a Daughter in Christ! She leverages her life experiences and sometimes own difficult lessons to help others bridge the difference between the lie of the evil one and the profound, irrefutable and foundational truths of God.

Her skills in Leadership stem from 25 years in Organizational Management, Training and Development and Business Analytics. Through her gifting of public speaking and presentation, she captivates audiences with a unique style and an infectious enthusiasm! While she supported strategic visions and executed against them successfully, she rose up other Leaders. She regards true discipleship as an organic byproduct of relationship and strives to enhance this aspect throughout her connection to God's people. Concurrently, she spent the last decade in active ministry, serving in multiple leadership positions and participated in church planting and expansion.

She earned a Christian Leader's Certificate from the globally recognized Bible Training Centre for Pastors and seeks a Divinity Degree from Christian Leaders Institute. As she answered God's call to the Pastorate in 2016, she began targeted preparation for her ordination in June 2017. She currently holds a Director assignment at a local church's Women's Ministry and supports the vision of its leadership as an Associate Pastor.

In remaining committed to her convictions, Sandra recently made a bold faith move and changed vocation to full time Ministry. God's leading and favor in this direction has since yielded numerous opportunities for both her ministry and also for her family. She quickly gives all glory to God for the continued strength, revelation and under girding as she submits to His will not only for her life, but also for the lives she is entrusted to!

For more information visit:
www.daughtersinchrist.com

www.ingramcontent.com/pod-product-compliance
Lightning Source LLC
Chambersburg PA
CBHW071357290426
44108CB00014B/1578